Prai

HOW TO COMMUNICATE
WITH THE DEAD

"I love this book! It is so hopeful, entertaining, and also wise. Western society has conditioned us to see death as a disappointment and dying as a failure. But in many cultures around the world, death is a portal to greater awareness, an awakening of the soul, and our dead become our advocates. In this beautifully-written, engaging book, travel writer Judith Fein carries us on adventure after adventure into the heart of life's most potent mystery: death. With a kind of breathless joy and ample moments of humor, she describes the many ways people connect with the ones they love who are no longer in this world, filling us, the readers, with a surge of hope that we too can continue these precious relationships after our own loved ones have died."

Mirabai Starr, Author of *Wild Mercy* and *Caravan of No Despair*

"In my counseling practice I work with people who are grieving the loss of a loved one. I find Fein's technique for contacting the dead helpful for clients who feel unresolved. Having lost both my parents as a child I have found her guidance an important healing tool.

Fein is a global traveler, humanist, humorist, visionary, teller of tales, writer, and guide. In *How To Communicate With The Dead*, Fein describes her preternatural global adventures. She explores how other cultures perceive death and talk with their dead. She gently guides readers to access their own experiences, complete unresolved relationships, allow insight and permit release from the grip of grief. In addition to being helpful it's a fascinating, entertaining, unusual read."

Andrea Campbell, PhD, Santa Fe, New Mexico

"In this entertaining and inspiring book, Judie Fein leads us on a journey of inner and outer discovery. We travel to some of the most profound spiritual locations in the world to witness sacred rituals for connecting with the dead. Along the way Fein shares her own perspective on these experiences and offers practical, easy-to-learn methods anyone can use to speak with their departed loved ones. The mix of exotic locales and down-to-earth spiritual wisdom was an absolute pleasure to read."

Carolyn Marie Wilkins, Professor, Berklee College
Musician, Author, Psychic Medium and Spiritual Healer

"This was a fascinating read! Judith Fein's *How to Communicate with the Dead* is really a manual for communicating with the Living: the nondual oceanic Reality in whom we live and move and have our being (Acts 17:28). When we talk with the dead we are talking with persons or personalities, but eventually we realize all beings are manifestations of the One Being who I call God."

Rabbi Rami Shapiro, author of *Surrendered, the Sacred Art*

"Judith Fein's book *How to Communicate With The Dead* is a splendid cornucopia of delight, that reveals itself little by little as the very best stories do. It holds profound lessons for us all, coaxing us to look again at who we think we are."

Tahir Shah, author of *The Caliph's House*

"I love Judith Fein's writing. It seems to speak directly to the reader's heart. It is a great comfort to learn from her that around the world the veil between life and death is considered to be thin, and that we can communicate with those who came before us to connect, find resolution, ask questions, and ease grief. And our descendants will be able to communicate with us. This book is a page turner, and it pulls you in from the first line."

Sally Fisher, M.D.

"Judith Fein, a peripatetic gadfly of death, takes readers on a magical worldwide tour that raises questions about our deepest beliefs concerning the afterlife. She speaks to the dead. She observes the wildly varying cultural practices of death. And she insists that it's all a normal part of life. Read this and you'll never whistle fearfully past a cemetery again."

Bill Tammeus, journalist; former president, the National Society of Newspaper Columnists.

"As Judith Fein travels to places here on earth, with her heart, eyes, and mind wide open, she discovers the innumerable ways people from old and new cultures communicate with those who are no longer here on earth. She understands energy and shares her knowledge though the multi-ancestral, multi-cultural wisdom she encounters worldwide. She invites the reader to accompany her. As we travel and learn from her, she destigmatizes — in fact, normalizes — the practice of communicating with those who have died. As we all search for meaning and connection, and a sense of belonging in a time when so many of us feel isolated and question a true purpose in life, having access to our ancestors can help us to feel a sense of continuity and perhaps, find meaning.

I hope everyone reads this magnificent book. It is a resource for those who are looking for ways to help them through challenging times. These times can be related to the passing of a person or not."

Dr. Dale Atkins, Psychologist. Expert in all media. Co-Author: *The Kindness Advantage*: Cultivating Compassionate and Connected Children

"As a Psychologist, much of my work has involved grief. In the past year and a half I have been the Clinical Director for a University Of South Florida study at Hospice in Clearwater Florida. Working one on one with the survivors of loss I find the dead ever present in the loss. With complex grief, the relationship with our loved ones is suspended in such pain that it stalls one's ability to grieve. Our work moves one through the pain until the whole of the relationship comes into view. Recently a woman told me of something humorous her husband would have appreciated. She asked me, 'Is it okay to talk with him?' It was as if she had been waiting for permission to speak with the man who had shared 50 years of her life.

Judith is a bright guide along the road for many of us. She shares her experiences with teachers, holy men, priests and shamans– those who stand as guides between this world and the next. If you are willing, she can help you to connect with your history and with those who have gone before us."

Dr. Diego Hernandez, Psychologist, Clinical Director Military and ART Research; University of South Florida, College of Public Health

HOW TO COMMUNICATE
WITH THE DEAD

And How Cultures Do It
Around the World

This book is dedicated to everyone who has thought about mortality.

How To Communicate With The Dead
And How Cultures Do It Around The World
By Judith Fein

Copyright © 2019 Judith Fein

A GlobalAdventure.us book
P.O.B. 31221
Santa Fe, NM 87594
https://www.GlobalAdventure.us

Printed in the United States of America
Cover design by Anne Clarke
Back cover photos by Paul Ross

INTRODUCTION

Dear Readers,

For the last four decades, I have traveled around the world, experiencing how other cultures communicate with the dead. For a very long time I didn't reveal that I, too, communicated with the dead. In my culture, and in my professional life as a travel journalist, death was something you didn't talk about. But I was exploding with the desire to tell others about what I had seen, heard, and experienced.

A few years ago, I wrote an article explaining one way for people to communicate with those they have lost, and I was stunned by the response. Hundreds of thousands of readers found their way to it, and many hundreds contacted me directly. They came from the U.S., the Philippines, Australia, Europe, Asia, North and South Africa, the Middle East. They were students and scholars, artists, lawyers, moms, dads, bereft siblings. They were curious. Skeptical. Afraid they couldn't do it alone. They asked if it went against their religion to want to be in contact with their departed. They needed reassurance that they weren't crazy. They were afraid evil spirits would rise up and harm them. They had suffered profound loss, recently or long ago, and they yearned to be in contact with their loved ones. Sometimes they were angry with someone who had died and wanted to tell him or her. Some were desperate to reconnect to the loves of their lives that had died tragically. There were things they needed to know from those who had passed. They had hundreds of questions and I tried to answer every email. I was touched by each story, and could not ignore the pervasiveness of the desire to maintain contact with those who have died and to know that death is not the end of contact with the living.

I decided it was time to take people on an adventure with me as I crisscrossed the world. I want to share with others the thrill, the mystery, the excitement, the brilliance I have experienced of how cultures everywhere connect to their dead and what they believe about an afterlife, reincarnation, and the non-linearity of time. I want to tell it to you exactly the way I experienced it. It has enriched my life immeasurably and made it multi-dimensional. I feel like the chains of learned perception have fallen off, and I have seen things I never dreamed of or considered before. I want to share it with you.

If and when you begin your communication, you will have the confidence to know that you can do it and that people all over the world do the same thing. Without knowing it, you may be surprised to learn that you are already doing it. You will also know that when your time comes, you, too, will be able to communicate with the living.

Death is not an end. In many ways, it is a beginning. So let me start at the beginning....

PART ONE

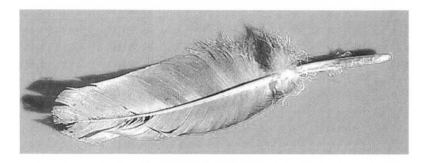

Chapter I.

VISITING DAD AND
SUSPENSION OF DISBELIEF

When I was 20 years old, my father, who had never been sick, died at age 50 of glioblastoma, a pernicious and fast-growing brain cancer. I was haunted by his death, and by the horrifying details of his three-month march from vibrancy to the tomb.

It was somehow comforting to visit the cemetery in New York where he was buried. His grave seemed like a focal point, a place to go when I wanted to connect with him. Sometimes I would tell him, in my mind, about struggles I was having at home. If he were still alive, he would have answered me, but that was no longer possible. Other times I stood staring at the small plot of earth, and tears cascaded down my face. How could the man who had been present in my life from the moment I was born, who taught me to swim and to waltz, who visited me at college to check out my boyfriend, who called me his fair-haired daughter, be lying under the ground?

When I saw people my own age in the street laughing, talking, playing, flirting, I felt like they inhabited a different universe from me. They had fathers. All of them had fathers. They were carefree. I was overwhelmed by loss, death, and grief.

One afternoon, in mid-summer, I went to the cemetery, and was standing in front of my father's grave when I heard a male voice say to me, "Don't give up your writing either." I spun around, but no one was there. I figured I had imagined it. But the voice continued speaking. "Take care of your mother, and tell her I am okay."

I fumbled in my bag, found a pen and a scrap of paper, and wrote down the words exactly as I had heard them. Then I sat in my car for a long time, thinking about what had happened. It was the word "either" that startled me. Either what? If the voice spoke in my imagination, it would have used words the way I do. But I would never say, "Don't give up your writing either." I wouldn't have structured the sentence that way. I wouldn't have used the word "either" unless it was comparing one thing to another thing. I only knew one person who might have voiced those words, and he was dead. I was really confused and perturbed.

I drove home, trembling inside, and called my older sister to tell her what had happened. She didn't seem a bit surprised and said to me, in a very matter-of-fact tone, "Of course he spoke to you. You were open. You were ready."

I didn't sleep very much that night, and when the early rays of sun stretched out like extended fingers that reached the foot of my bed, I was still going over the words, "Don't give up your writing either." Why shouldn't I give up my writing? I had been writing since the age of five, and was first published in my school paper when I was nine. I had written plays, short stories, poems, song lyrics, essays, theatre and movie reviews. But I had decided to go for my PhD, and become a scholar and a professor. I was starting a PhD program in the fall. I was going to study and teach college simultaneously. Why was my father telling me not to give up my writing?

In retrospect, it turned out that my father was right. I enjoyed teaching and loved my students, who were only slightly younger than I was, but being immersed in bibliography, critical writing, and endless research was clearly not my calling. I quit after several years in academe, and became a writer. Thank you, Dad.

But back to the cemetery. It took a while for me to accept that my father was speaking to me from the other side. Eventually the new reality became part of my existence. The death of my father had been like someone pulling away the *terra firma* that I had stood on before, and underneath me there was only shaky ground. I no longer felt safe. I inhabited a universe that had become ominous and incomprehensible. But in spite of my feelings, I still went on with my life. And dating was part of that life. I changed relationships like clothes, and my father was part of the reason for my fickleness in love.

Every time a man wanted to get serious, I asked him if he would agree to meet my father. The answer was always yes. They obviously thought they were going to visit my parents' house. Instead, I directed them to the cemetery, and asked them to drive inside the gate and park. Then I walked them to my father's grave. I smile now as I think of how strange the experience must have been for them. I asked them to please leave me alone and walk somewhere else in the cemetery.

Once they were gone, I inquired of my father, "Well, what did you think of him?" The answer was immediate, detailed, and negative. Once my date came back to the graveside, I looked at him a little differently, and sooner or later it turned out my father was right.

Years later, I fictionalized these cemetery visits in a short play called 'Visiting Dad.' It was about a woman who asked her boyfriend if he would meet her father, and he agreed. At the gravesite, the father not only spoke to the daughter but to the man as well. He saw through the prospective suitor, unpacked all the secrets he had been hiding, and berated him soundly. In the end, though, he kind of liked the guy and said he'd make his daughter happy.

The play won an award, was published in a prestigious collection of short plays, and I still get royalty checks from performances. Obviously, other people in my country and other countries could relate to the story of communication from the other side.

And then I moved away from New York. Cemetery visits were no longer part of my life, but my father still was. His gravesite was replaced by…how should I say this…a portable place where we could communicate.

I had been raised in a Jewish household and although I was not religious, I certainly remembered many of the practices. One of them was the *yahrzeit* candle. On the anniversary of someone's death, you lit a candle for her or him that burned for 24 hours. It was a candle-in-a-glass, and it had Hebrew writing on the outside. My grandparents burned *yahrzeit* candles for their parents, and my parents lit candles when their own parents died. Each time they purchased a new *yahrzeit* candle, it was spiritually burnished from generations of tradition.

One year, on the anniversary of my father's death, April 7th, I lit a *yahrzeit* candle and was about to set it on the kitchen counter when I saw the flame dancing in the glass — moving side to side, then growing smaller, and suddenly leaping up again.

In a flash, I knew what to do. I carried the candle over to the table, sat down, addressed my father, and began to communicate through the medium of fire. Wow. It worked. I purchased *yahrzeit* candles at other times, unrelated to the anniversary of my father's death, and it always worked.

One night, I had lit a candle and was talking to my father. The phone rang and it was a friend of mine who called from Los Angeles, needing advice. He said he had an urgent question to ask me. I told him that I was afraid I couldn't speak to him right away as I was talking to my father through a candle in a glass. My friend, who is usually very logical and skeptical, must have been desperate. "Hey," he said, "Could you ask your father to help me out?"

It seems crazy now as I write this, but it seemed natural at the time. I took the phone receiver, put the part of if that contained a microphone inside the glass with the candle, and told my friend to ask his question. I heard his voice coming through the phone, and then I saw the flame bouncing, almost frantically, inside the glass.

I interpreted the flame for my friend, said the answer to his question was a definite NO, and then hung up. He later told me that he had been on the verge of resigning from his job at a Hollywood studio, and it would have been a terrible mistake. He thanked my father for the advice.

Over the course of the next decade or so, I told a few children who were grieving that there was a way to contact the dead, if they were willing. For all of them, it was their first contact with death, and they were anxious to connect to their beloved grandmas and grandpas. Two of them later told me that the experience changed their attitude towards death for the rest of their lives. They had been devastated by the loss of a grandparent but learned that the grandparents were still accessible.

Then I offered the information to a few friends of mine who had experienced loss and were suffering terribly. To my surprise, one of them said she was too afraid to do it, and another said she wouldn't do it because she didn't believe in it. I was surprised because it seemed so normal to me and I couldn't imagine anything to be afraid of. The worse case scenario was that it wouldn't work.

Other friends were able to contact those they had lost, and it offered them great solace.

And then my mother began a slow descent towards death. When it was clear that she wouldn't rebound, I asked her if she would be willing to arrange a sign with me — something that would tell me she was still in contact after she died. I gave her a few examples: heads-up pennies, a particular song, or white feathers. My mother frowned and put an end to the conversation. She said she had no interest.

But after she died, especially when I was going through a difficult time, white feathers appeared everywhere. At first I thought it was a coincidence, and I was attributing the feathers to my mother rather than to the birds that had shed them. But then some unusual things happened.

My husband Paul had an attack of gout in both feet and knees that left him in pain and unable to walk. He is a strong, athletic man who couldn't take three steps. I found the name of a medical supply store in a small strip mall and headed over there to get him crutches. The salesperson said I should come back in half an hour. I was worried about my husband, called him several times to make sure he was okay, and then walked over to a nearby market to get something to eat. When it was time to return to the store, I noticed that the cracks in the sidewalk were filled with white feathers. I was sure they hadn't been there when I walked to the store, but there they were.

As I approached the medical supply store, I saw what looked like a large web in front of the store next door, and it was filled with white feathers. I snapped a photo, because I thought no one would believe me.

Another time, I was out of town, and had just gotten some bad news. Paul suggested we go for a walk around a nearby pond, and I agreed. When we arrived at the pond, there were about five brown ducks swimming in it. As I was watching the ducks, Paul grabbed my arm and said, "Look!" He pointed off to the other side, where I saw clumps of white feathers, but no white ducks.

We walked around the pond on a concrete walkway, and I said to Paul, "If this is real, then we'll see a white feather at the end of this concrete walk where our car is parked."

And there it was. A single white feather lay on the concrete walk near our car. My mother, who was a contrarian, would not consider my request for a sign when she was alive. But after her death, she made her willingness quite clear. And although she was not demonstrative in life, she was reaching out to help me after her death.

The white feathers were real. Not only could the dead communicate with words, as my father had done, but they could communicate through objects in the physical world. All I had to do was be open and pay attention.

Chapter II.

NIGERIA AND A RINPOCHE

A long time ago, when I was living in Europe, I had a Lebanese Druz boyfriend. His father Arif, whom I adored, had been a visionary businessman who was heavily invested in Nigeria. But he had suffered a severe stroke, which greatly impaired his mobility and necessitated him living permanently in Europe to get medical treatment.

My boyfriend, the eldest son, had to go to Nigeria to oversee some of his father's affairs and I went with him. I was plunged into a world that was as fascinating as it was foreign and chaotic. I dined with wealthy international businessmen and CEOs, and naively asked them and their spouses if they wanted to come with me to local events, museums, and markets. There was zero interest. So, undaunted, I went alone. Nobody was interpreting or mediating the experiences I had. I was a blank slate, and the Nigerians were writing on it, teaching me, imprinting me with rich cultural traditions and customs that were very different from my own.

I fell in love with the women who laughed as they tried to braid my baby-fine hair into cornrows, and the Yoruba people with facial scars who carried their tribal identity on their faces. I adored learning Pidgin English expressions, like "*he day like he no day.*" It meant, "He's there like he's not there." You certainly know people who are "*no day,*" they are physically present, but their minds and attention are not there. They "*day like they no day.*"

One sultry night, my boyfriend and I were invited to dinner at the home of two wealthy Lebanese Druz brothers. When they waltzed out to greet us, their handsome, creamy-brown skin and casual, elegant, long, white robes dazzled me.

Dinner was a multi-course affair, during which Nigerian servants carefully and silently placed each dish on the table. It troubled me that the brothers never spoke to the servants. They ignored them or gestured imperiously to them.

After dinner we retired to the living room, where I tried to bite my tongue, but it kept eluding my bite and finally I blurted out, "Why don't you speak to your servants?" The men shrugged with indifference. The conversation turned to other things, including reincarnation. I knew very little about the Druz religion because it is fairly secretive and esoteric, but I knew that Druz are big believers in life after death. The brothers spoke animatedly about incidents when young children went to villages and knew what had happened there decades before they were born. The children could identify rooms in the houses where they used to reside, and talked about what their lives were like.

The brothers said they were not afraid of death because they would be reincarnated.

"And what if you are reincarnated as black Nigerian servants?" I asked.

There was a horrified stillness in the room, only punctuated by the whirring of the overhead fans.

The brothers, clearly disturbed and perplexed, conferred privately. Finally the elder of the two spoke aloud. "It would be impossible for us."

"Impossible? Why is that?" I inquired.

"We will never come back as black Nigerians because you can only reincarnate upwards. You can't go backwards," the elder brother replied, as his younger brother nodded his head vigorously in assent.

It was distressing to experience such colonial ignorance and assertion of superiority, and I was secretly glad that I had shocked the brothers. But I was grateful for my first encounter with people who believed in reincarnation and claimed to have proof of reincarnation, and I would never forget it.

Several decades later, when I moved to Santa Fe, New Mexico, a very generous couple we knew invited Paul and me to attend an event at the Paolo Soleri Amphitheater, which had been built in the 1960's. It was formed from a bowl-shaped depression in the earth, and the bleacher-like seats spread out in a semi-circle that faced the stage. Luminaries like Lyle Lovett, Leonard Cohen, and Carlos Santana had performed there.

But we were invited for a very different event. It was a Tibetan Buddhist performance and, as I recall, it included not only Tibetan Buddhist monks, but nuns as well. Our friends were avid supporters of the Tibetan Buddhist people and were friendly with His Holiness the Dalai Lama.

We arrived early, and the couple was already there. I smiled when I saw the woman running through the bleachers, as I used to tease her about never getting exercise. It was curious that she was running after a young Tibetan boy, who seemed to be about four years old. "Rinpoche, Rinpoche," she was calling to him. The child kept running, and my friend kept pursuing him. "Rinpoche, please, come back!" the woman exhorted him.

A Rinpoche is an incarnate lama or highly respected religious teacher. Why was my friend addressing him that way? When the young boy stopped running and finally bounded over to the woman, she explained to me that he was a reincarnated high teacher. She spoke with the respectful matter-of-factness that she would use to describe a beautiful flower, mountain, person or jewel. To my friend, reincarnation was a given.

I don't remember her exact words, but she explained that our lot in life is to come back to clean up the messes we have made with wrong thinking, behavior, feelings. It is not a choice; rather, it is involuntary. This is *karma*. Do something rotten, and you may get away with it in this life, but you'll have to come back and right it in the future. Also, there are some high beings that can decide, after they die, where and when they want to return, and to which parents they will be born. They are called *tulkus*

She went on to explain some of the mystical ways a child is identified as a reincarnated being, and I recall being dumbfounded that another culture accepted reincarnation so easily, while we could barely talk about death.

A few years later, I attended the graveside service for a man who was very important in the Cathedral Basilica of St. Francis in Santa Fe. I didn't know him personally, but I had spoken to him on the phone and was an admirer of his and the work he did. He had suffered a lot before he died.

As expected, many people gathered around the deep hole that had been dug for him, and his body lay in a coffin on a bier, ready to be buried. But I didn't expect what happened next. The priest concluded the service and suggested that people might leave at that point. Within minutes, everyone had departed, except for a few family members of the deceased.

I stood at a distance, watching, trying to understand. When someone we care about dies, shouldn't we accompany that person and bear witness until his or her last minutes on earth? Couldn't we bear to be with the deceased until he was in the ground? Did we need to be shielded from the sight of a body in a coffin slowly being lowered and then covered with dirt, until we couldn't see it any more? I wondered if people who gaped into that six-foot hole to eternity, imagined, with a terrified shudder, that one day the dirt would fall on top of them. And perhaps they recoiled from the idea of finality, mortality, and being no more. They would never again see the sun dappling through the red, gold, purple, and yellow leaves of trees in their autumn splendor or hear the soft sound of snow falling in winter. They would never laugh with friends, fall in love, hold hands, touch the cheek of an infant, read a book, walk, sigh from the first bite of a perfectly crisp apple, sing aloud in their cars with the windows open, or gaze upwards at constellations and galaxies.

I remembered the words from Genesis, when God threw Adam and Eve out of the Garden of Eden. It was the end of innocence and immortality. Humans would have to work, women would have to bear the pain of childbirth, and one day they would die. The King James Version described the inevitable arc from birth to death lyrically, and the words have inspired poets, singers, and artists: "In the sweat of thy face shalt thou eat bread, till thou return unto the ground; for out of it wast thou taken: for dust thou art, and unto dust shalt thou return."

I thought about the skulls, clocks, hourglasses, and evanescent flowers in European Renaissance paintings, and the medieval Christian theory and practice of *memento mori*. Remember death. The objects that represented the passage of time were invitations to contemplate death and the transience of life, and to understand the uselessness and vanity of attachment to the material world. When you are aware of death and you remember how impermanent this life on earth is, you begin to appreciate more deeply and fully the fact that you are alive. You take nothing for granted, because you know that one day it will vanish. All around us, all the time, are reminders to look, see, feel, taste, pay attention to little things. We can stop and listen to the caw of a raven on the highest branch of a tree, and appreciate the perfection of a golden apricot that tumbles into our palms as we pluck it. We can imagine that the brook is bubbling and gurgling for our pleasure, and allow a song we hear on the radio to ease our pain. We are visitors in this world, on this planet, and one day we have to say goodbye. We can cherish and relish what we have while we have it because sooner or later it and we will be no more. We all share this privilege and this destiny.

I also knew that if the Druz brothers and the Buddhists I met were right, then death is nothing to dread. His Holiness the Dalai Lama said that he tends to think of death as being like changing clothes when they are worn out. Death is not an end. Your body will be gone, but your soul and your energetic essence will live on. You may come back, and then come back again and again, each time in different apparel.

Death is a gateway to something else. We get glimpses and reports from people who have physically died and resuscitated, we hear about the supernal light, but we may never know exactly what happens after someone dies. We get to open the cookie jar and look inside, but the cookies are forever beyond our reach. What happens after the soul sheds the body may be one of the ineffable mysteries of life that we can guess at and are not meant to know. But one thing I knew for certain from my own experiences was that the deceased live on in another form. We may not know or understand the realm that they pass on to;

that knowledge will be given to us when we, ourselves, expire. But we can still retain connection to those who were close to us after they die. We have the ability to contact them, and they are able to contact us. We may be contacted spontaneously, without initiating anything. We can seek out the guidance, help, and forgiveness of the dead, and the dead may do the same with us.

In many ways, the dead are as anxious to communicate as the living. And they have their ways....

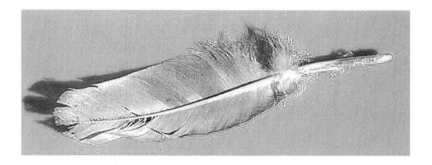

Chapter III.

HOLLYWOOD AND LIGHTS

When I was a Hollywood writer, a lot of time was spent going to meetings. In my experience, there was a sameness to all of it. You get your ideas together, you dress up like an adult, you drive to someone's office, you sit in the waiting area and chitchat with the receptionist or assistant, you are ushered into the producer or studio executive's office, you are offered something to drink, you make small talk, laugh on cue, try to be clever and charming and animated, and then there is a sudden change of energy in the room, a lacuna, a gap in the conversation, and you know it is time to pitch. You launch into enthusiasm mode, punctuate your sentences with exclamatory excitement, compare your idea to other successful films or TV shows, and expend a lot of energy trying to connect the person across from you to your idea.

Occasionally you get real, actionable excitement, sometimes you get vague interest, other times you are asked to change it to suit the person you are talking to, and sometimes you get turned down on the spot and skulk out of the office with your emotional tail dragging between your proverbial legs, but you still act cheerful.

Somehow, and maybe it had to do with the kind of subject matter I was interested in and pitched, I had a bit of a reputation as a spiritual person — whatever that means. To me, spiritual refers to how you treat other people on a minute-by-minute basis, and how you conduct yourself in the world with your fellow *Homo sapiens* and other sentient beings, but let me get back to the story.

Roxanne Captor was one of the women I pitched to a few times. She was a smart, hard-working producer, but, like everyone else, if she liked your project she still had to go and sell it to other people so she could get a deal. We went to lunch once or twice and she seemed quite interested in spiritual realms. All I knew about her background was that her mother was French and her father Italian.

One day I got a call from Roxanne's assistant. She said, "Roxanne wanted you to know that her father died and she would like you to come to the wake." I asked her to please give Roxanne my condolences, and said that of course I would come. When I hung up, I realized I had never been to a wake before.

It took place in the chapel of a funeral home within walking distance of my house, and Paul and I arrived at the appointed time. The wake was like a visitation and a viewing of the deceased, and it took place before the funeral. Because I wasn't familiar with Catholic funerary rites or how one was supposed to behave, we sat at the back of the chapel out of respect.

When we had settled in, someone came up to me and said Roxanne would like me to come to the front of the chapel. Paul and I walked towards the platform where Roxanne's father was lying in an open casket and we were about to sit in the front row when the same person whispered to me, "Roxanne would like you to come onto the platform and do what you know how to do."

Do what I know how to do? As I wondered what the words meant and what was expected of me, I walked onto the platform where Roxanne and her mother were standing next to the coffin. Paul sat down in the front row.

As soon as I saw Roxanne's father, I was so comfortable that I leaned my elbows on the edge of his casket and began talking to him and, more important, listening to him.

Out of the corner of my eye, I saw Paul motion to me, but I had no idea what he wanted. I continued chatting with Roxanne's dad. Paul was, by then, making desperate signs to me, and finally he came up to the stage and whispered to me. Apparently, I was so comfortable with Roxanne's dad that I was leaning heavily on one side of the coffin and the other side was raising up and in danger of toppling off the bier.

I was mortified, and put less weight on the coffin, but I was thoroughly engaged in what Roxanne's father was communicating. He said that he would make his presence known to his family within 24 hours and would tell them, through lights, that he was okay. When I reported this to Roxanne and her mother, the latter seemed mildly freaked, and she looked at me as though I were an alien life form that had plunked onto the platform from another planet.

I stepped down from the stage, and shortly afterwards, Paul and I left.

I had some regrets about what I did. I wondered if my mind had conjured the voice of her father and invented a message to make Roxanne feel better. Maybe the whole thing was the product of a febrile imagination and had no basis in reality. I hoped I hadn't ignited false hopes.

Several weeks later, Roxanne called and said she had to talk to me. I braced myself in case it was something negative that she had to say.

She reported that after the service they had gone to her parents' house. Family and friends came to pay respects and offer condolences, and when they had all left, Roxanne, her mother and her husband were in the living room watching TV when all the lights, the television, and everything else electronic went dark. It was exactly the time frame her father had laid out: 24 hours after we had been on the platform together at the wake.

"My husband said that it was probably a power outage, and, sure enough, within a short time, everything went back on," Roxanne continued. "He checked the fuse box, and everything was fine. Later on, when he went to ask the neighbors if they, too, had experienced a loss of power, none of them had."

Roxanne took a deep breath, and went on. "At exactly the same time, we got a call from some non-profit organization. They wanted to know if we would be interested in buying a set of light bulbs that came six to a package, as they were raising money for people who became handicapped as adults by events like a stroke. My father had been handicapped by a stroke. The light bulbs were very cheap, like a few dollars, so I told them yeah, sure, I would buy a pack. The person at the other end of the line sounded like an older woman. Her voice was very calm."

Roxanne hung up the phone after the solicitation and it rang again. Someone wanted to confirm that she had just placed an order with an organization that helped handicapped adults by selling light bulbs. She said yes, she had made the purchase.

"I hung up and went back to the living room. One of the light bulbs in the adjacent dining room popped out and fell to the floor. No one was even near it," Roxanne reported. "It just popped out of the socket and landed on the floor. I was never billed for the light bulbs, and they never came. I checked up on the organization, but couldn't find out anything about it. Maybe it never existed. It all happened 24 hours after the wake, and we knew it meant my father was okay, that all was well with him."

Before writing this, I decided to contact Roxanne to verify the facts and make sure I had her permission to use her name. She was traveling in Europe, and said I should call her the Saturday after she returned home. She sent me her current phone number, as we hadn't spoken in over 20 years.

Saturday came, and I was distracted by phone calls and emails. In the afternoon, Paul and I wanted to get out of the house. I got dressed but before we could leave a storm broke out. Rain was pouring off our roof, the earth seemed to shudder with each growl of thunder, and zigzags of lightning flashed across the sky.

"Since we can't go out right now, I think I'll phone Roxanne," I said to Paul. I sat down at the kitchen table, and before I could pick up the phone to call, it rang. It was Roxanne. "I was just about to call you at this very moment," I told Roxanne. "I'm not surprised," she said.

We spoke, and she confirmed the story of what happened after her father died. As I listened, I felt the presence of a man standing behind me, on my right side. He was short and had a round face.

"Roxanne, I don't recall...how tall was your father?"

"Five foot eight."

"And his face...can you remind me what shape it was?"

"He was heavy. His face was round."

"I think he's happy you told me your story and I am writing about it," I said.

"I'm glad to hear that," Roxanne said.

After the call, Roxanne's father vanished. He had a purpose, he appeared, and then he left. There was nothing spooky or frightening about what happened. He was a physical presence who showed up, briefly, when he had something to communicate. I had never seen the physical manifestation of a dead person before. I didn't feel that he contacted me because I was in any way special. I was simply a conduit that could deliver a message to his daughter. At his wake, he spoke from his coffin. From whatever realm he was in at the present time, he was able to appear as a fleeting apparition.

Maybe the dead have the ability to communicate when they are needed, or when they have something to say to the living, or when someone is remembering them.

Now that Roxanne's father had stood behind my right shoulder, I had experienced each one of these things. All I had to do was be receptive.

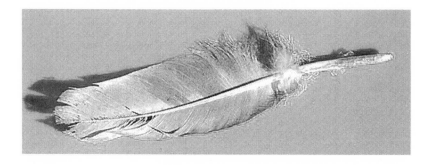

Chapter IV.

YAP AND MOG MOG

As a travel journalist it has been my good fortune to travel around the world, and experience how birth, marriage, death, communicating with the departed, and the afterlife are viewed by different cultures. If I am receptive, people talk to me. When I'm open and curious, it's like holding a prized ticket to events that are difficult for outsiders to access.

Some years ago when I was on the island of Yap, in Micronesia– 9,394 miles from New York and 6,883 from Los Angeles – I made a request of the locals with whom I spent time: "Do you know of anyone who just had a baby, is getting married, or who has died, and wouldn't mind if I attended their ceremony?"

They shook their heads. Undaunted, I asked every person I met, but the answer was always the same.

"How about the outer islands? Any life ceremonies there?" I asked.

I was informed that the outer islands were remote and largely inaccessible. Every few months, a boat named the Micronesia Spirit came to Yap to transport folks to the islands, but there was no fixed schedule. If you happened to hear about a crossing, you could book passage. Otherwise, there was no way to get there. A few expats who lived on the island of Yap said they had never been able to visit the outer islands, even though they had tried.

Just as I was about to give up any hope of witnessing a life ceremony, the manager of the hotel where I was staying knocked on my door. "There is a funeral ship going to the outer island of Mog Mog," she declared, beaming, "and you are booked on it. Congratulations!"

When I told some locals of my good fortune, they turned ashen. "Hasn't anyone warned you about the Micronesia Spirit?" they asked. I shook my head and laughed.

Two days later, at dusk, I stood at the pier. I watched as a coffin was solemnly carried onto the three-tiered boat and then I boarded the Micronesia Spirit with a rolled-up yoga mat, a sandwich, and two bottles of water that the hotel manager had given me. The ship, licensed to transport 150 mortals, was dangerously over-crowded with close to 250 passengers. It seemed that everyone but me had staked out a place to sleep, and most were already lying on overlapping woven mats or flattened cardboard boxes so that the decks were a human carpet. I'd been told that you never step over a prostrate Micronesian, so how could I walk around the ship without stepping over bodies? I stood still and plotted what I would do to get through the next fourteen hours. Finally I decided to retreat to the lower deck and settle near the coffin. After all, I couldn't offend the dead.

All night a group of women encircling the coffin sang as I was drenched by waves crashing over the side of the dangerously overloaded ship. I was sure I wouldn't make it off the boat alive until a kind Micronesian man named Brodney approached me. "Do you need help?" he asked gently.

Frightened and exhausted, I gazed at him and, smiling sweetly, he offered me a large loincloth. I thanked him and stared at the decorated length of material, wondering if I was supposed to strip and wrap it around my loins before swinging from the ship's mast like Tarzan? I felt dumb and dumbfounded.

"Okay?" Brodney asked. I raised one soaked eyebrow.

Taking this to mean "yes," Brodney deftly twisted the loincloth into a hammock that he suspended from two nails. Then he helped me climb inside. At last I felt safe, and I closed my eyes. Suspended above the deck in a gently rocking loincloth, I would finally catch some winks. Five minutes later, the rains came —pelting thick ribbons of water that drenched me and Brodney's loincloth.

Fourteen hours after leaving Yap I arrived at Mog Mog, where I encountered topless girls in grass skirts and men wearing loincloths. Only the fourth outside visitor in a year, I was chided for changing my shoes on the steps of what turned out to be the sacred men's house. I hobbled across sharp stones until my feet bled. A few locals took pity on me and invited me to their outdoor cooking areas where they offered me fresh fish, taro, stew, and as much coconut water as I could drink.

Eventually, I camped outside the house where the coffin lay amid the ritualized crying of grief-stricken women. As they wailed, they also expressed their feelings about the deceased — which were not always positive.

A man from Mog Mog, who acted as my translator, said mourners might talk about the generosity of the deceased and also his drinking and abusive behavior. They can praise his skills as a storyteller and regret his periodic irresponsibility and lying to cover up for his wrongdoing. They can lionize or lambaste him.

At first I was shocked. Can't they just leave the dead in peace? I wondered. But I said nothing, sitting and listening to the wailing and talk.

Finally, fascinated by the idea that people speak their truth about the deceased but not quite understanding how and why it is done, I asked my translator.

"During a Mog Mog funeral," he began, " people are expected to air all of their feelings about the deceased person publicly, so the negative emotions don't eat away at their insides. The bad feelings are expressed, rather than kept inside, and then they are buried along with the body. At a funeral, people reveal their true feelings, but speaking badly of the deceased outside of this context is taboo. And it is forbidden to speak badly about the dead person once he is lying in his final resting place."

"You mean that a person doesn't become a saint just because he had died?" I asked.

"He can be a saint. He can be a sinner. He can be both. And maybe it is a relief for the person to die without any secrets."

The funeral experience and my translator's explanation resonated with me on a very deep level. Perhaps the inhabitants of Mog Mog got it right. A person doesn't automatically ascend to sainthood just because he has left the earthly plane. Maybe honoring a person for what he did right or wrong during his lifetime isn't a bad idea. It may actually be inspired. And perhaps it gives peace to the soul of the person who has died. No more secrets. No more lies. No more shame. Everything is transparent, out in the open. And it is done publicly.

"The people who are left behind express who the deceased really was, and with that open truth there comes a relaxation of tensions that are kept inside. So saying the truth brings a kind of peace for the living and the dead," my translator explained.

"It's good," I said to him, and he nodded.

Then I noticed a man who had come over with me on the Micronesia Spirit. First he said hello, I said hello, and then he said he was happy to make my acquaintance. I said I was happy to make his. His face was so open and friendly, that I inquired if it was appropriate to ask him a few questions. Yes, he said.

"Do you believe there is life beyond our life here on earth?"

"Oh yes," he said with conviction. "There are spirit worlds. Certain people can communicate with spirits, for sure."

"And do you think the deceased person can hear what is being said about him at his funeral service?"

"Oh, yes."

"And can it bring relief or peace to the living and the dead?"

"Yes, for sure, ma'am."

I didn't ask any further questions, and he didn't provide any more information, but I had learned all I needed to know. Even if the relationship was troubled, the living can help the dead by speaking the truth and telling the real story. It is a weight removed from the hearts of those who continue living, and even absent any forgiveness, it allows the deceased to acknowledge what he did that was wrong.

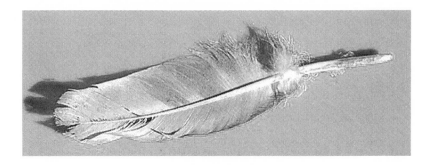

Chapter V.

SAUL GOES UNDERCOVER

O ne of the earliest stories I have encountered about someone who made serious mistakes and reached out to connect to the dead is found in the Hebrew Bible. It may surprise you to learn that Jewish people have a long and complex history of communicating with the dead.

In the Biblical narrative, Samuel was a much respected and admired prophet in the period before the monarchy began in ancient Israel, about three millennia ago. He received a divine message to anoint Saul as the first king of Israel, because the people were demanding a king like other nations had; they wanted someone who could save them from their enemy the Philistines. Among his other attributes, Saul stood a head taller than anyone around him — which, I presume, may have referred as much to his character as his height. Or maybe his height was his best characteristic. In any case, Samuel anointed him, and told him all that would be required of a king according to divine and human law. When Samuel died, he was greatly mourned and had he lived, he might have regretted elevating Saul to such a high status.

Saul revealed himself to be seriously flawed; he disobeyed divine law, and ultimately found disfavor with God. One of his acts was to ban all magicians and mediums from the land. But before a major battle with the Philistines, he needed wisdom and could not obtain it from dreams or prophets or God. He asked his servants to find him a medium, even though he, himself, had banned them. He disguised himself and he was taken to the woman (sometimes referred to as a witch, but actually a seer) of Endor. Because of his disguise, she did not recognize him as the king.

He asked her to descend into her ritual pit to summon up a spirit from the dead. I always imagined this to be a pit that was lower than the level of the ground, and that was somehow mystically or spiritually connected to the underworld or world of the dead. The woman became afraid that her visitor wanted to trap her and get her killed for disobeying King Saul's order against necromancy. But the disguised king promised her safety and she agreed to summon the spirit of the dead he asked for: Samuel.

When Samuel's spirit was called up and began to speak, the woman understood that her visitor was King Saul himself, but he reassured her again of her safety. Samuel's spirit was annoyed at being disturbed but Saul said he needed help and advice for his battle with the Philistines, and that God had turned against him. Samuel predicted Saul's defeat and demise.

The woman felt sorry for Saul and offered him food, but he declined. Finally, he was urged to accept the victuals by the woman and his servants. The woman sacrificed a calf to feed him and made him bread. It was to be his last supper.

The next day, Saul and the Israelites were defeated on the battlefield by the Philistines. Saul saw three of his sons slain from his high vantage point on Mt. Gilboa, and when his servants refused to honor his death wish, he killed himself. Samuel, called up by the witch of Endor, had accurately predicted the battle's tragic outcome for Saul. He lost it all – kingship, sons, and, ultimately, life. Would Saul's end have been the same if he hadn't consulted with the woman of Endor? Or was it Saul's inescapable destiny?

When I visited Beit She'an in northern Israel, I climbed the hill where Saul's body was hung along with his three sons after the battle. It was pretty chilling to stand there, where it all happened.

Some people I know have taken the story of King Saul as an illustration of the danger of consulting with spiritual mediums. They believe a medium can suggest an outcome, which might push a person into a dangerous situation or even death. They are also worried that a medium can call up evil dead spirits that will harm them. One woman I know is plagued because a relative of hers cursed her shortly before expiring. She is terrified that the spirit of that relative can hurt her if she is called up.

I asked my friend Andrea Campbell, a highly trained and insightful therapist, what she thought about that, and her answer was, "A curse can become self-fulfilling. For instance, the person who has been cursed first feels guilt, anger, or shame and as a result of these strong emotions gives power over to the person who was the ill wisher. Thus they become receptive to the curse and often sort throughout their lives for evidence of the sting of the curse; it's like sorting through dirty laundry. There are more creative solutions like writing a letter to the ill-wisher and then burning it to let the smoke be a symbol of release. You can ask supportive friends to witness your ceremony. You may also immunize yourself by treating yourself with compassion and vowing to forgive yourself when you make a blunder. Start imagining what it would feel like to be free of the curse. Recognize the amount of energy it takes to hold onto a grudge until the grave. Imagine what an impoverished choice the curser made by using her or his energy this way, especially at the end of life."

One of the reasons I am writing this book is to share with you many options you have in dealing with people who have left the earthly plane. I invite you to contact the departed by yourself, without anyone else intervening. When you initiate contact, you are in control and you have the power to shape the conversation. You can start it when you wish, and end it when you wish. If it is disturbing to you in any way, you can stop the connection. If it is helpful and soothing, you can make it as long as you desire. Communicating with the dead is a shimmering, private, healing act that can ease and transform loss and resolve confusion and conflict. You can start it or cease it at any time. You may decide not to do it at all. You can do it with someone who has been dead for months, years, or decades. You can confer with other people to see what they think about you doing it. But, ultimately, it is about your relationship to a loved one or an unloving one who is deceased, and, if you wish to try it, it is a way you can contact that person in a heart-to-heart, intimate setting. Your brain may conjure up worries and dangers, but you are in control, and I suspect the dangers are in your mind and not in reality. Contacting the dead is an act of love, even though there may be unresolved conflicts and issues with the departed.

Samuel was called up by Saul and he was irritated because it was against his will. He responded to Saul's request, even though he didn't want to be disturbed. Communication with the dead is a kind of contract. There is an initiator and a recipient. Both parties have to be ready and willing. If one does not want to communicate, it is necessary to back off until the time is right, or accept that not all the living or the dead want to be contacted. Just as in life, sometimes a person doesn't want to talk or communicate. She or he may want to converse at a more propitious time, or not at all. We have to respect that. Talking with the dead is like talking with someone who has feelings and thoughts but no longer has a body. The deceased person you contact is an enhanced version of the person you knew, but with more wisdom, humility, and insight. They are no longer trapped in denial, ignorance, judgment, fear, or anger. They are, perhaps, consumed by regrets, which is the reason they choose to contact you. They did something or many things that were awful here on earth and they want your forgiveness. You are not obliged to give it, but it may provide solace to you to know they have remorse. They may beg for love and understanding, and it is entirely up to you to say yes or no.

When someone does something awful, people often say, "I hope he rots in hell." I have never been able to relate to a heaven or hell, but if there is a hell, it is probably someone's after-death awareness of what he has done, and the inability to rectify it. That is why many cultures believe that people come back again to get it right.

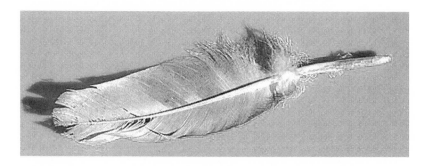

Chapter VI.

TUNISIA, MANAUS (BRAZIL), UKRAINE

In contrast to the sad story of Saul in the Hebrew Bible, I have witnessed wonderful, joyous, healing take place in the present, with both secular and very religious Jews, when they contact the dead. I'd like to tell you about a few of these experiences.

The island of Djerba, in Tunisia, an Arab Muslim country in North Africa, is home to what perhaps is the oldest extant Jewish community in the world. Oral tradition says the first Jews came as traders as far back as Kings Solomon and David, which would mean 3,000 years ago. They certainly came after the destruction of the first temple in Jerusalem by the Romans in 586 BCE. Many of them are descended from the Levites, the priests in the ancient temple. Until modern tourism with its hotels, spas, and importation of contemporary clothes, behaviors, gadgets, relations between the sexes, and cultures, they were cut off from the outside world and preserved ancient customs.

In the street, Muslims bring chickens they have raised to the kosher slaughterer. A Muslim man bakes bread on the Sabbath, when Jews are not permitted to work. And Muslims attend the festivities on major Jewish holidays. Jews are famed as goldsmiths and silversmiths, and many of their best clients are Muslims. Besides Judaica, they also sell Muslim pieces.

The spring holiday of Lag B'Omer is a time of pilgrimage to Djerba for Jews from Tunisia, Israel, France and elsewhere. They come to this very conservative, religiously observant and closed community, where men and women are rarely seen together in public, and foreigners are not usually welcome.

But all of that changes for two days every spring. Lag B'Omer marks a break from the solemnity of a 49-day mourning period. It is a raucous, joyous holiday and, surprisingly, in a patriarchal culture, it's about a woman. Her name is the Ghriba. Her exact identity and the date of her death are lost in the mists and vapors of time, but she was beautiful, alone, and the inhabitants of Djerba paid little attention to her, so she lived a solitary life of isolation.

One night the Ghriba's house burned to the ground, and when the Djerbans found her the next day, her body was unblemished. They understood then that she was a saint. Muslims honor her too.

For Lag B'Omer , the Jews build a wooden structure called the *Grand Menarah* and parade it from the synagogue, which is called the Ghriba synagogue, through the streets. It is adorned like a bride, and sprayed with perfume.

Under the synagogue is an earthen cave where the Ghriba's house was said to be. During Lag B'Omer , women crawl into the cave on their hands and knees, holding raw eggs. Each one is inscribed with the name of a woman friend or relative who needs to meet her beloved, or is unable to have children. The egg is left overnight, where it cooks in the heat of candles, which are placed in the cave. The next day the women come back, crawl into the cave to retrieve their egg, and give it to the woman whose name is on it to eat.

You could perhaps think all of this is superstition — making an offering to a person long deceased to help a woman in need. But I met women who said the benefits of asking the Ghriba for help were very concrete.

"I never met the right man for me, and I suffered in a lot of bad relationships. I began to think something was wrong with me and I would never meet the right kind of man," a teacher from Paris told me. "But after I asked the Ghriba, I met my soul mate. We got married, and it was all thanks to the Ghriba."

"For two years, I couldn't get pregnant," a young mother said. "My husband and I were very sad and we were ready to try artificial methods, but then the Ghriba helped me after I had given up hope. And she did the same for my cousin."

"A patient of mine had intense back pain that didn't respond to any treatment. Her activity and her life were severely restricted. After she came to ask the Ghriba for help, her back pain became minimal and she goes about her life pretty normally now," a doctor said. After a slight pause, she continued. "So I decided to ask the Ghriba for myself. I was widowed eight years ago, and I couldn't shake my depression and feeling of hopelessness. After I came here last year, I found a *baguette* (French bread) relationship. It was the last baguette in the grocery store and we both wanted it at the same time. He said I should take it. There was something about him that seemed almost familiar. We started to talk and it's a long story, but a happy story. We are getting married and he accepts my feelings about my first husband and doesn't feel threatened. I came back to thank the Ghriba."

In the Amazon rainforest of Brazil, in the city of Manaus, a rabbi who has been dead for over 100 years is still performing miracles, according to local Catholics. They call him "Santo Rabino," and consider him a saint.

On the day I was there, the tomb of Rabbi Moyal was surrounded by candles that were placed there by Catholic followers. They also left plain stones, which is a Jewish custom when one visits someone's grave. I was intrigued by the rabbi's supposed afterlife powers and asked the Catholic guardian of the cemetery about him.

"He is a miracle worker," the affable man said. "This morning I left my house, locked the door, and realized I had forgotten to take my wallet. When I looked for my key to get back into the house, I couldn't find it. I searched every pocket, the ground around me, everywhere, but no keys. I was really getting nervous about how I would get into my house. When I came to work, there was only one solution: I had to ask Rabbi Moyal for help. I lit a candle and begged him to help me. He did. I found my key, and am so grateful to him."

I became very curious about how the rabbi became a miracle worker, and heard various stories. In all versions, he came from Morocco to minister to Amazonian Jews. And in 1910, he died from a fever, which was either yellow fever or malaria. At that time, there was no Jewish cemetery in Manaus, so he was interred in the municipal cemetery.

It was later decided that the rabbi's remains should be disinterred and sent back to Morocco. Or, alternately, his body should be put to rest in a Jewish cemetery in Manaus, which was established in 1920. But a terrible thing happened to each man who was tasked with digging up the coffin. According to one version, all of them died from mysterious diseases or accidents.

The Jews of Manaus seem to be quite accepting of the fact that Catholics have sanctified a rabbi, and concur that he has effected many miracle cures.

In southwestern Ukraine, I was surprised by what I found near the tomb of Rabbi Nachman of Breslov, who died more than 200 years ago. Within the city of Uman, a little Jewish town had grown up. The curb of the steep main street was lined with artists and vendors selling Rabbi Nachman-inspired paintings, crafts, and books.

During the rabbi's lifetime, he made the esoteric teachings of Kabballah and the deep meaning of the Torah available to anyone who was interested. He stressed humanistic values, hope, hospitality and helping others. One of his core teachings is called *hisbodedut*—talking out loud to God, as though one is having a conversation with a best friend. And, fittingly, many pilgrims come to the rabbi's tomb and speak to him as though they know him personally and ask him for help, blessings, and spiritual guidance.

I opened the door to the women's side of the building, and saw a playpen for babies, dozens of *tsedaka* (charity) boxes in all shapes, sizes, and colors, and bookshelves lined with prayer books; I selected a thin, paperback one, and smiled when I saw that the cover art was a fiddler on a roof. I was wondering why, exactly, people traveled from far away to go to the rabbi's tomb, and a young woman from Israel must have heard my thoughts. She explained to me, in perfect English, "In the synagogue, God is abstract, and hard to reach. There's nothing to see, to touch; you just have to believe. But a tomb is something physical. And inside is one of God's ambassadors. It is a way of getting closer to God. People come here who are very religious and others come who are not religious at all. Even if you have tried to get pregnant for ten years without success, you can come here and have a miracle." I wondered if that was why the young woman had come. And when I overheard her talking to Rabbi Nachman, that was, indeed, what she asked for.

The tomb itself was covered in black material with gold Hebrew lettering; on top of it was a protective plastic layer. Prayer requests, written on small pieces of paper, were taped to the top of the tomb. A young woman with a baby daughter in her hands sat next to the sepulcher. She must have felt me approaching behind her, because she turned and smiled. I noticed that she was elegantly dressed in a long black skirt and the hair of her raven-colored wig caressed her face and cascaded down her shoulders. Like other Hasidic, Orthodox, and ultra Orthodox married women, she wore a wig to cover and hide her hair, which might be sexually arousing to men other than her husband.

She held up her baby daughter so she could touch the tomb. Another religious woman rocked gently as she read from a prayer book. Then she leaned her head on the tomb, and I heard her soft sobs as she asked for healing.

Before I left the room, a young woman approached me with an outstretched hand, asking for *tsedaka*. I told her I had already made contributions in two boxes. "Please help me," she implored. "I don't have enough money to run my household. Rabbi Nachman will open the gates for you." I gave to her, hoping that indeed, the gates would open.

Because Rabbi Nachman was a *tsaddik* or spiritual leader in life, because his teaching elevated humanity, it was believed that he had a special relationship with God. He could, like Moses in the Bible, petition God directly to ask for help for the people. The pilgrims who came to Rabbi Nachman's grave were asking him to intervene on their behalf. In life, he was a kind of an emissary of God. In death, his soul is elevated, and he is even nearer to the divine.

I have seen people in both religious and secular contexts asking extraordinary dead people to help them. On some level, I think many of them have a sense that connecting to an exceptional person who is dead will somehow elevate their requests and perhaps their lives. If the person who died is considered holy, they may pray for miracles, healing, and divine intervention in trivial or important matters. They ask the dead for favors for themselves and their loved ones. They often recite prayers, which is a way of praising and giving back when they are asking for help.

Some people travel to the tombs of great masters like Rembrandt or Mozart and ask for artistic inspiration. They sometimes petition dead sports figures, world leaders, dancers, writers, healers or those who excelled in almost any area of life to give them courage, fortitude, victory, physical or emotional strength. And if they feel their request was answered, they give thanks to the departed and sometimes return to the tomb where they petitioned. It is a way of giving back.

I believe that in all communication with the dead, it is necessary to give back, in the form of gratitude, honoring, or any other manifestation of appreciation. Sometimes all that is needed is a simple "thank you" when the communication is done. You thank them for showing up. Maybe, like Samuel, they didn't want to be disturbed. But you asked, and they showed up. A sincere "thank you" is a simple, beautiful payback.

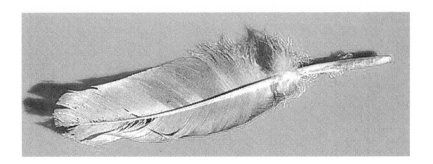

Chapter VII.

KWAZULU NATAL IN SOUTH AFRICA

My husband Paul, ever a skeptic, nonetheless had a healing experience with a dead person — actually multiple dead people, which began when our plane was about to land in South Africa. He started experiencing extreme pain in his ear. Even after we landed, his ear still hurt, and finally we went to a doctor who said his eardrum had almost burst, and he wouldn't be able to take a flight home.

So we extended our trip in South Africa, and Paul took the antibiotics and steroids that were prescribed, but the pain in his ear persisted. It didn't stop us from delighting in the deep culture and people of South Africa, but it was distressing to see how uncomfortable Paul was.

Finally we decided that we had to go in another direction, both metaphorically and literally. With a Zulu-speaking guide, we went to

Kwazulu-Natal to find a *sangoma*, or native healer. She trained the other *sangomas* in the area, and locals raved about her powers.

We entered a hut where she was performing a ceremony, surrounded by drummers and attended by acolytes. She didn't look at Paul, but she picked up a mortar and pestle, mixed some herbs, and drank them. Immediately her voice became deep and otherworldly. In a jerky movement, she lifted her hand to her head and cupped it around her ear. Then she looked straight at Paul and spoke. Our Zulu interpreter translated what she said. "You think your problem is your ear, but your problem is that you don't know how to connect to your ancestors. You must perform a ceremony and invite them into your life."

Then she gestured for Paul to come forward and stand next to her. She took a red yarn-like thread and wrapped it around his torso, draping it over his shoulder and tying it. She told him he had to wear it for several months, as I recall.

Paul, who is not woo-woo and doesn't indulge in magical thinking, grew very silent as the *sangoma* told him exactly, precisely, how to make a ceremony to invite the ancestors in. It involved colored candles, the gate of our house, and speaking their names.

Paul spoke in a low voice to the healer. "I don't know anything about my ancestors — not even their names," he confided.

"It does not matter," she said, slowly and clearly. "But you must call them in."

She said he could do it in South Africa, and then when he got home. He nodded his agreement.

Paul kept the red string on at all times, except when he showered. And he planned his ceremony. He invited a few men to be part of it, and he performed it at the gate of the hotel where we were staying. He became a bit emotional when he called out to his deceased ancestors, asking them to come to him, and to help him. He said he realized what a loss it had been to grow up with no connection to his forebears; it had been discouraged in his family.

"I felt, for the first time, that they were not just grandparents and great grandparents and great-great grandparents; they were also people who were once young, and had hopes, dreams, aspirations, joys, and sadness. They had loved and lived, and then they had passed on, and no one spoke their names or remembered them," he told me. "I thanked them all, even though I don't know their names. It didn't seem to matter. I just thanked them."

After the ceremony, Paul went to sleep. When he woke up, his ear was healed.

When Paul told his doctor about what had happened, the latter said there was a much more rational explanation: the ear infection took longer than expected to heal. Sometimes that happens. The medication doesn't work at first, but it facilitates healing over time. It wasn't the *sangoma,* the ancestors, or the ceremony that healed Paul. And he added that healers can be dangerous, and ancestors are nice, but they don't affect healing.

Rational explanation. I wanted to open my mouth and say what I was thinking, but I refrained. What was the use? The doctor was trained, he had experience, and he was just giving Paul his best shot at a logical explanation. He was a kind man who meant well. But to me, his thinking was very limited and limiting.

What I wanted to but didn't say was that the rational brain is necessary and very useful for many things in life, and none of us would be happy if we couldn't think, but I have come to believe that sometimes thinking can also be a reflection of mental imbalance. We go over and over what-ifs in our minds. We think with regret and anger about the past and create fearful scenarios about the future. We think about all the mistakes we have made and how incompetent we are. We think we are inferior or superior to other people. We think about how others think of us, and that we have nothing important to say. We think that people who annoy us are doing it on purpose. We think that we have to behave, act, dress, and talk in a way that conforms to the expectations of others. We worry, fret, anticipate, and dwell on things that are harmful to our wellbeing. Thinking about solving a mathematical problem, studying and learning any discipline, fixing something in the house or car that is broken, the meaning of a poem, how to help someone, why the sky is blue, a funny joke, choosing a good restaurant for dinner, the book we are reading or film we are watching, planning a party, going on vacation, calling a friend, what to say on a job application are good uses of the brain.

But there are ways of thinking that lock us in, prevent us from being open to new experiences, make us disbelieve things that are not explainable through reason, lead us to scorn or reject things that are mystical, supranatural, or defy rational explanation. And when this happens, we are the losers. We cut ourselves off from wonder, mystery, and deep experiences that can transform our lives. We have nothing to lose by asking "what if?" rather than slamming the door in the face of the non-rational with a resounding no. No, it's not possible. No, it's not real. No, it's not for me.

Paul, who is an inspired, creative, and very rational being, who has no interest in organized religion or organized spirituality, who doesn't go out looking for experiences or people that are mystical, who distrusts anything that he deems "misty moisty," nonetheless accepted an offer to reach across time to ancestors he hardly knew, communicated with dead people, and was healed. And recently he agreed, when prompted during a talk about death and dying, to write a letter to those grandparents he never really knew. I didn't read the letter, I don't know its contents, but I knew from the deep exhale he emitted after writing it and the smile on his face moments later, that he felt satisfied, perhaps relieved, and connected.

Chapter VIII.

A NIGHT IN SALVADOR DE BAHIA

I n Salvador de Bahia, Brazil, I had an inexplicable experience with the dead several decades ago that lives on inside of me with such intensity that it's as though it happened a few days ago.

Paul and I hadn't come to Bahia for the beaches. It was the Afro-Brazilian culture that appealed to us, and the influence of the Yoruba tribe of Nigeria. I wrote earlier that I had lived for a while in Nigeria and found everything about the tribe fascinating, from their facial scarification to their brilliant drumming, beadwork, and their possession by spirits called *Orixas.*

While we were having breakfast in a small restaurant, I noticed an old, torn, water-damaged, dog-eared guidebook on the bottom rung of a bookshelf, and I began to leaf through it. There was a footnote to one entry, which stated that November 2 was *Dia dos Finados,* or Day of the Dead, and there was a special celebration on an island that was about an hour from Salvador. It was November 1st, and I was determined that we had to get there the next day.

As we walked past the magnificent colonial architecture in the city, I stopped everyone I could, asking if he or she could tell us how to get to the island. The one-word response of each person was the same, "*fechado*," which means "closed." We talked with people of every age, shape, and color, with poor people and rich people, with police officers and hucksters, and the response was always the same: "*fechado*." I gave my journalistic credentials, handed out business cards, and said I wanted to write about it. *Fechado*. At some point, I gave up and, exhaling a deep sigh of disappointment, accepted that some things were not meant to be.

You can probably surmise what happened next, after I let go of all expectations. The following morning, the phone rang in our hotel room. I picked up the receiver and a male caller said, "I hear you are interested in going to *Dia dos Finados* on the island. Is that correct?" I could barely contain my joy. "Yes, yes, yes!" I enthused.

"Here is what is going to happen," the man said. "I am going to go to the island to ask the priest if you may attend. It will take me an hour to get there by ferry. Then I will come back to Salvador and call you. Be at this phone at 3 p.m. If the priest says yes, we will leave shortly after that."

I never asked the man who he was, or how he knew where we were staying. I just followed his instructions.

We explored Salvador all morning, and at two thirty Paul said, "Let's go back to the hotel, just in case he calls early." Then he looked at me tenderly and added, "I hope you won't be disappointed if the priest says no, or if he doesn't call at all."

It seemed like the latter was going to be the case. At 3 p.m., we hovered near the phone, but there was no call. At 3:30, we were about to leave the hotel room when the phone rang. I pounced on it. "The priest said yes," the male voice reported. I will come by for you in half an hour. I will meet you in the lobby."

We had no idea who was meeting us, what his motive was, what we should bring or wear. We showered, washed our hair, put on fresh, light-colored clothes, and waited in the lobby. At 4 p.m., the front door of the hotel opened, and in waltzed a tall, handsome fellow with smooth, cocoa-colored skin and Hollywood-leading-man looks. I think his name was Roberto, and we introduced ourselves as we followed him out of the hotel to the ferryboat terminal. When our ferry arrived, we boarded after him.

For the entire duration of the ride, we spoke about mundane things. He never mentioned the ceremony. Neither did we. And we never asked a single question. We instinctually felt that we shouldn't.

When we arrived at the island we disembarked, and Roberto led us to a steep, dirt hill, and gestured for us to climb it. Paul and I exchanged a sidelong glance, and we began to climb. The dirt was loose and the only way to climb was by using my hands and feet and kind of crawling upwards. It was extremely humid and we were both sweating profusely. My hair was matted and stuck to my face. I wiped it away and kept climbing.

When we got to the top of the hill, Roberto led us to a dusty, outdoor area where about 15 people were sitting on wooden benches and folding chairs. No one acknowledged our presence, and we certainly stuck out because we were the only white people. I found being ignored to be oddly reassuring, because it indicated that whatever we were going to experience would be authentic because no accommodation was made for tourists or visitors.

The sun was setting, time passed, but no one spoke to us. When they talked to each other, the language was familiar to me. "Are you Yoruba?" I asked one man who had facial scars. He nodded yes. "From Nigeria?" He nodded again. "Lagos?" "Yes." I felt as though I was back in Nigeria, in Africa, but it seemed like I was with Nigerians hundreds of ago, before their intense urbanization.

At some point, a man walked by, cracking a whip in the air. He paraded back and forth, from one side of the sitting area to the other.

"This man keeps the dead away from the living," Roberto explained to us. "It is a very important job. The Baba Egungun ceremony is going to take place tonight. The *egungun* are male ancestral spirits."

A woman and a man led Paul and me to a huge, shed-like building that was largely empty inside. The woman took me to the area for women, on the left, and the man showed Paul the space on the right for men. They beckoned us to sit down. It was odd that no one else was in the hall. By this time, I could see through one of the open doors that the sun had set completely, and the sky was dark. All at once people began to stream into the building, with the women heading to where I was sitting, and the men walking towards the men's side. The woman who sat next to me said, "Once all the doors are closed and locked, you cannot go out all night." I nodded agreement. "And the toilet is over there." She pointed to a door to our left.

Then the doors of the building closed with a series of loud thuds.

A few heavily draped, mysterious figures in voluminous bright textiles and face coverings manifested at the front of the hall, and began dancing and chanting or speaking in what seemed like other worldly, almost childlike, high-pitched voices. They did not have a human form, but I knew that under the mounds of textiles they had to be human masqueraders. Everyone watched them intently, and I didn't think it was appropriate to ask the women around me what was happening.

Then the mood changed entirely. What sounded like a group of men outside the building began to bang ominously on the front door, trying to get in. They shouted and pounded. Then they moved to other doors around the building, and the tension increased as they pummeled the doors in an attempt to break them down or force them open. Their voices sounded threatening and mean. The din got louder and louder and became a cacophony of yelling and banging and what sounded like the lashing of whips. I looked around to see if the women close to me seemed frightened. Their heads sank low between their shoulders, and they averted their eyes. I thought the anxiety-producing drama outside would go on all night. When it was almost unbearable because of its persistence, it suddenly stopped. Everything became very still. The women next to me looked up and adjusted themselves in their chairs. I wondered if the whips were used to keep the dead away. Who had been banging on the doors? Where did they go?

By this time, I was ready for a short bathroom break. I walked to the door of the only bathroom and stood in line. When it was my turn, I couldn't do it. I am not squeamish, and I have been in situations where I used every conceivable type of human-made and nature-made restroom, but the heat and humidity, the sheer number of bodies, the overflowing toilet and its contents were more than I could bear. Trying to suppress my gag reflex, I bolted from the room.

By some miracle, Paul was standing on line, and I quickly told him we had to get out of the building to go to the bathroom outside. He was surprised, as he had never seen me refuse a bathroom before. I grabbed his hand, and we made our way to the main door of the building. Two burly men were guarding it. I begged them to let us outside. They conferred, and then they went to talk to another man, and finally decided that we could go out, but we couldn't come back in.

This was a very difficult moment. We knew we were witnessing a rare ceremony, but, on the other hand, we both needed to heed nature's call. Finally Paul nodded, and the door was quickly opened so we could step outside before it slammed behind us.

The sky was tarry black, but enough moon shone on the hillside for us to find a secluded spot. I was about to crouch down when a blanket-shaped figure flashed by us, from left to right. I smiled inwardly, knowing it was someone in a costume trying to scare us. But when it flew by again, from right to left, it turned to the side, and it was no more than a few inches wide. No human could fit inside that blanket. I screamed involuntarily. Paul's eyes were the size of swimming goggles, but he made no noise. I shrieked again. A man appeared with a whip and chased the spirit away. Then he turned to look at us, saw we were okay, and departed. The blanket-shaped figure did not return.

It took quite a while for my heartbeat to settle down. After all, a spirit of the dead had just chased me on a hilltop on a remote island in Brazil.

When we came back home, I told a few Nigerian drummers who live in Santa Fe about what had happened. They were amazed, and said that this kind of ceremony hadn't been performed in Nigeria for many, many years. But on that island in Brazil, it was still going on. "Yes," one of the Nigerians told me, "You were very lucky to have that experience."

I heartily concurred.

After the Baba Egungun ceremony, it never occurred to me to try to "figure out" what happened on that hilltop. My rational mind was satisfied that I hadn't invented the experience because Paul also saw a large, thin "thing" flying by, but it would be useless to try to explain what the "thing" was. So I said I was chased by a spirit of the dead, encountered many raised eyebrows, but offered no further explanation.

At the beginning of the story, I reported that when I let go of any expectations, Roberto called with an invitation to the ceremony. And when I let go of trying to understand the hilltop event, I was open, primed, and ready for the next extraordinary experience that was to occur in Brazil, just as we were ready to leave the country.

Chapter IX.

SEEING IS BELIEVING OUTSIDE OF RIO

O f all the countries I have visited, Brazil has the most varied, deep, widespread belief in other realities and interactions between the dead, the spirit world, the gods, and the living. I met *Spiritists* who said they follow the path of Allan Kardec, the Frenchman who taught about immortality, reincarnation, and communication between spirits and humans. And I spoke to many people who were followers of Afro Brazilian religions like *Umbanda* and *Candomblé*.

One night a taxi driver was excited that I was interested in the religions and practices of his country, and he took Paul, three friends, and me back to his family house at midnight to see elements of the religion his mother and aunt practiced. They brought out elaborate costumes to show us, and spoke to us about the small wooden boat that hung from the ceiling and transported spirits.

It was liberating and thrilling to go to ceremonies in out of the way places, and experience the many ways Brazilians relate to the seen and unseen world around them. But nothing came close to what happened in a warehouse in a poor district on the outskirts of Rio de Janeiro the day of our departure from the country.

The story actually started many years before when I read the book *Arigo: Surgeon of the Rusty Knife* by John G. Fuller. It was the true, gripping story of a peasant in Brazil who had a third grade education, no medical training, wrote arcane prescriptions in German, diagnosed people without examining them, and treated hundreds of thousands of people using no more sophisticated tools than a kitchen knife and a pocket knife and, as I recall, operated on a horizontally-placed old door. He claimed that, in a trance, he became the incarnation of Dr. Fritz, a German surgeon who died in World War I. Skeptics said there was never a Dr. Fritz.

In 1968, a team of American doctors went down to observe Arigo, and his psychic or spiritual surgery. They documented, photographed, and observed the truth of what had been reported: using no antisepsis or anesthetic, Arigo was performing surgeries and healing people from high government officials to local farmers. He was arrested, jailed, and hundreds of people lined up to be healed by him when his jailers opened up the back door of the jail so he could treat them.

I think the fact that his work had been observed and photographed by American doctors gave the story credibility for me. And I wished that I had known Arigo when he was alive. I tried in vain to get Hollywood producers and executives interested in the story. I showed them the book about Arigo, I gave each of them a treatment for a movie, but my idea was met with laughter, incredulity, or general lack of interest.

One time, I heard that a Filipino psychic surgeon had come to Santa Fe. I was intrigued, because I thought he was someone who worked like Arigo. I booked an appointment and was impressed with the vigor, dedication, and powerful energy of the man. But my treatment was a disappointment. At the end, he produced, in a cup, a blackish wad that he said he had removed from inside of me. "You are such a powerful healer," I said to him. "Why do you have to use magic to show me what you extracted?" The man threw up his hands and said, "Because people need to see tangible evidence." "Could you do psychic surgery without producing that evidence?" I asked. "Yes, but people wouldn't believe…"

Fast forward to many years later, when I heard there was a new incarnation of Dr. Fritz in Brazil. This time, it was an engineer named Rubens de Faria, Jr., and like Arigo he had no medical training but was healing legions of sick people, many of whom had been declared hopeless.

I decided that I would not leave Brazil without meeting Rubens de Faria, Jr., and it happened on our very last day. Our plane was at night, so I knew we would have time to get to the warehouse in the poor outskirts of Rio where he saw his patients.

Outside of the huge storehouse, people lingered and chatted. I asked a few of them what they knew about Dr. Fritz, and they yanked up their shirts and blouses and pulled down the waist of their pants to show incisions he had done when he removed their gallbladders, goiters, and other diseased body parts. Each one said how long ago the surgery had been — in most cases, years. When I asked if there had been anesthesia, they said no. Pain? None. Were there infections afterwards? Heads turned from side to side.

Paul, who had been pre-Med when he was in college, was highly suspicious. But we were both very, very curious about what we would find inside.

The doorway to the warehouse was open, and when we entered we saw many hundreds of people lined up, patiently, waiting. They seemed undeterred by the humidity or heat.

We walked to the front area, said we were journalists and had been following Rubens de Faria, Jr. for years. We were ushered into an area that looked like an office. Faria had his head down, hands folded in front of him on his desk, and I think he was praying. Then he lifted up an x-ray, quickly scanned it with his eyes, and handed it to a female assistant.

We were introduced to Dr. Fritz, a handsome, dark-haired, friendly man, who said we were welcome to observe his healing. Then he walked into the large room and an assistant followed him, pushing a cart that had bottles of liquid and needles. As he greeted each patient, he was handed a needle.

I asked another assistant what was in the needles, and she said, if I recall correctly, "alcohol and iodine." "Couldn't that kill you?" I whispered to Paul. "I think so," he answered.

We watched from a distance as Dr. Fritz started at the front of an extremely long line, chatting to patients, and injecting them. No one died on the spot.

An ambulance arrived outside the warehouse, and a woman was carried in on a stretcher. Her abdomen was quite distended, and her skin had a gray, almost blackish hue. Dr. Fritz approached her, and felt her belly, looking for a point of entry. When he found it, he inserted a needle and drained a liquid. The woman lifted her head and thanked him. Then she was carried away.

Unfortunately, Paul had to leave because it was approaching checkout time at the hotel and he had a 45-minute drive to get there. We quickly arranged that he would come back at the end of the day to pick me up, and we would drive right to the airport.

I decided to ask one person standing on line if I could follow him. I chose a tall, thin, dark-haired man with bushy eyebrows, baleful eyes, and horn-rimmed glasses. He wore a white T-shirt and shorts. He said his name was Miguel, he was 42, and he had been impotent for more than a year. He was hoping that Dr. Fritz could help him. He said it was all right if I accompanied him for his treatment and didn't seem particularly squeamish about his ailment.

I wondered about how one man could treat what seemed to be close to 1000 people in one day. But as the line advanced, I saw how it was possible. Dr. Fritz spent about 20 or 30 seconds with each patient. My head was bobbing on its axis as I looked around the room at the people being treated, at Dr. Fritz, his assistants, Miguel, the patients on line in front of us and behind us. And all the while the line advanced and Dr. Fritz was administering shots.

Before too long, it was Miguel's turn. He told Dr. Fritz what the problem was, and the former stuck a large needle into the right testicle of the latter. I held my breath, imagining the pain and screaming that would ensue. But, on the contrary, Miguel and Dr. Fritz were talking and laughing while it was going on. And the liquid in the needle was gone.

As soon as Miguel left Dr. Fritz's presence, I asked him what he had felt, and he said he felt good, and had no pain whatsoever. I do not know if his impotence was cured or not, as he left the warehouse.

I stayed in the warehouse, observing Dr. Fritz for hours. I watched him giving injections and then I saw him doing spiritual surgeries with a real knife and real incisions on real people with lesions, growths, and internal pains. I saw him work on adults, teens, and very young children. I watched as another stretcher was carried in from an ambulance; the sick person had come straight from the hospital. At one point, I actually had to hold onto the wall, to brace myself, to be able to absorb what I was seeing. It was so beyond anything I had ever witnessed that I truly didn't know which compartment of my brain to put it in.

I watched more incisions made in flesh. It happened very fast. On arms, necks, backs. On eyes. Often there was no blood and sometimes there were a few drops of blood. There was no anesthetic, no antisepsis. And no one cried or screamed.

I did not see any exchange of money, at least from the people I observed. Or perhaps they gave money to someone elsewhere in the warehouse, but I did not witness it. I saw someone bringing a chicken for payment. I saw sacks of beans, corn, and other dried food. And most of the people in the warehouse seemed to be on the poor or poorer end of the economic spectrum.

It was helpful to talk to the assistants. One of them whispered that Dr. Fritz had injected himself with the AIDS virus, to see if it could run through him and heal others. Another said she was afraid he would kill himself from working 12-13 hours a day, and seeing up to 2,000 patients a day.

Before I left, I got video footage of Dr. Fritz performing surgeries to bring home with me. And I had a chance to talk briefly again with Dr. Fritz. I said I had read about American doctors who went to observe Arigo, and one of them had actually had surgery himself. I asked Dr. Fritz if he would agree to receive American doctors who could witness his work. He agreed readily, and said he would love to teach them. I said I would try to bring some to the warehouse.

One of the assistants asked me if I wanted a treatment. An injection. I thought for a moment, but I just couldn't do it. I was too concerned with hygiene.

As soon as I got home, I called a doctor friend, told him about the experience, and asked if he and a few other physicians he knew would be willing to go with me to the warehouse in Rio. He said yes, he would be happy to ask several of them. "Tell them, please, that if they are disappointed, they can spend a few hours there and then enjoy Rio and Brazil," I suggested.

I was unprepared for what happened. All of the doctors said they would go, but they had grave hesitations. Where were the double blind studies? Where were the articles in reputable journals? Had I done follow up with the patients? Had I stayed in contact with them? Did I have statistics? Did I know about infections?

I tried to explain that I was not doing a scientific or medical study. That I wanted them to go because they were doctors who are familiar with the kinds of surgical interventions Dr. Fritz was doing, and perhaps they would be able to learn and use his techniques, which he said were teachable. The back-and-forth went on for weeks, and finally I gave up. It was too difficult to bridge the gap between spiritual or psychic surgery and the American-trained physicians.

I learned that Chris Reeve, alias Superman, had gone to Rio to see Dr. Fritz, and so had Joao Figueiredo, the prominent Brazilian military leader who became the President of Brazil.

I lost sight of Dr. Fritz, but I read, in 1999, that he had been charged with, I think, practicing healing, having one patient who died afterwards in the hospital, and being sued by one man who claimed that after his treatment he was unable to perform his work. As I understand it, the case was dismissed for practicing healing, there was insufficient evidence to link Dr. Fritz to the patient who died in the hospital, and in the third case, he had to pay $25,000 and part of a minimum wage pension.

At that time, Rubens Faria, Jr. was going through an acrimonious separation from his partner, she accused him of taking $10-$20 from each patient, and he was outed in the press for making a million dollars. He continued to be hounded by media and official institutions, and his warehouse of healing was closed.

I wanted to know what happened to Rubens de Faria, Jr. and was able to contact him through LinkedIn. I told him I was writing a chapter about him, and offered to send it to him to make sure what I said was accurate. He agreed. He was friendly and open, and instead of summarizing our conversation, I thought you might be interested in hearing a few excerpts directly from him. I am not sure if he wrote in English or used a translation program, but I made some minor corrections when they were necessary to render his responses more understandable in English.

I asked him if he was still doing what I saw him do in the warehouse in Brazil.

His reply: I am still working in that way, but now I am a real doctor. I studied psychology, medicine in Boston, and I am PhD in Neuroscience. I did it all in an attempt to understand this phenomenon. I hope one day we can talk about it. Thank you very much for your important contribution to make our concept of faith and plurality of realities more clear.

I inquired about what happened after his problems and did he still incarnate Dr. Fritz?

His reply: After several years my lawyers proved that the accusations were not true. In matter of fact... the media was just making money with a family problem and not speaking about or explaining my work. Took me 10 years to get out of these stories and to prove my innocence. You were there and you know what you saw.

I am doing what I was doing... we need to go on our own path to understand ourselves, and God. I didn't stop believing in Dr. Fritz or in a spiritual way. I still work with him, doing the same things, but now I try to add all the information that I got from science and my goal is to use this to help more people. I have been in 39 countries, seeing a lot of healers doing the same thing in different ways. I have dedicated my own life not to spirituality but to helping and understanding people. I never was interested in the phenomenon itself...I was interested in people and what faith and belief could bring to us. I only wanted to understand those 2000 people every day and impart to them something for their lives. Something they could talk about with their children. I think science is a way to do this. I don't treat thousands of people any more, as I told you my path is in another direction.

I asked if he was available for healings or seminars.

His reply: I am looking for somebody to organize some events (seminars or healing) in the U.S.A.

Because of translation difficulties, I am not sure I completely understood what Rubens Faria, Jr. was saying, but I found the essence to be moving and intriguing. Science. Psychology. Faith. Multiple realities. Dr. Fritz. Spirituality. Somehow he was able to put it all together, modify the direction he was going in, and incorporate all of it into his life's work of helping people to heal. Instead of separating science from spirituality, he married them. Rather than choosing one or the other, he found a way to embrace both. He didn't pursue either spiritual or scientific studies as an end in itself; his goal was to enrich and expand his knowledge and skills so that he could be of service.

I admire the fact that his universe is not limited to reason (science) or mysticism but he is seemingly fascinated by both in an unlimited way. As a scientist, he acknowledges that some phenomena are ultimately mysterious and unknowable. As an energy healer, he feels that he also needs a foundation in science. And he continues to have fluid interactions with both the living and the dead.

"You know what you saw," he said to me several times during our correspondence. I do, indeed, know what I saw in that warehouse in Brazil. And in a way, I think that my indelible memory of it was a prelude to meeting other healers whose mystical gifts were given to them by people long dead. In one case, the people bestowed the gift almost two millennia ago. And it happened in Italy.

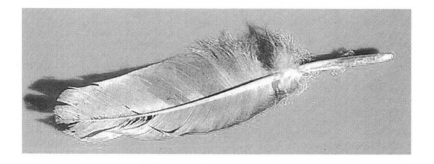

Chapter X:

ITALY: THE MAN
ON THE MOUNTAIN

In the region of Umbria, in central Italy, in the mountains above the medieval town of Spello and the nearby city of Foligno, there is a tiny village with a total population of eight. When Paul and I went there more than 15 years ago, we were told it represented a population explosion, because, until recently, the population had been a mere five. Surprisingly, there was a huge baroque church in the village, and locals said the church was built by "donations." They also referred mysteriously to the "father and son healers who live in Cancelli."

Maurizio Cancelli, who lived in the village by the same name, was a robust man of about fifty with wild hair, broad gestures, and a lively twinkle in his eyes. When I asked him if he was a healer, he denied it, although he acknowledged that people came from all over Italy for his help. When pressed, he agreed to tell us his most unusual story.

"Legend has it that the apostles Peter and Paul came through here two millennia ago to spread the gospel," he began slowly. "The Cancelli family lived here, and they were simple shepherds. There was an ancient town near here called Civitella, so it wasn't as out-of-the-way as it is today. Civitella was a walled city, and when the apostles arrived it was night, and the gate was closed."

Cancelli paused for a moment, and then continued his story in rapid-fire Italian. "So the apostles came to Mr. Cancelli and asked for hospitality. At the time, the Cancelli family lived in a hut, but Mr. Cancelli took the apostles in for the night."

In the morning, the grateful apostles did a service for Mr. Cancelli. He was suffering from rheumatism or arthritis and they performed a hands-on healing, in the tradition of Jesus. Miraculously, Cancelli was healed. The apostles told him that whoever had faith in them—and therefore faith in Jesus or God—would be healed.

"From that day on," Cancelli said, "the gift of healing has remained here in the village and has been passed on from father to son. But they have to live here. You see, the gift of healing is linked to hospitality and receiving people. They are permitted to travel, but if the person with the gift moves away from Cancelli, the healing just won't work."

Maurizio Cancelli was raised with this tradition. He learned the healing from his father, and he taught it to his son. "I say the prayer in Italian," Cancelli reported, "but I found out from my friend, a Benedictine monk, that the prayer was originally in Hebrew, and it was the prayer fathers said to bless their sons. This helped to validate the story about the apostles for me. It was a sort of proof."

Cancelli seemed like a down-to-earth man, who was taught the technique by his father when he was ten years old. He grew up, got involved with politics, city government, raising a family and developing his skills as a fine art painter, so he didn't have the free time or peace of mind to attend to the family legacy. Instead, he let his father and his own son carry on the tradition. "But now my father is old and his memory is gone. He can't do it any more. My son is 25 years old, and I hope he will stay here, but it's hard for him. We're in the middle of nowhere. So the responsibility lies with me," he said.

Every week, people sought out Cancelli for surcease from suffering and pain. He usually did his healing work in the church, which was entirely built from donations left by people who were treated. But the church suffered damage during an earthquake in 1997, and was closed for restoration when I was visiting. So Maurizio Cancelli worked in a wooden hut–which was probably closer in spirit to the kind of house the original Cancelli lived in.

Cancelli decided that he wanted to find out if the family legend was true, so he began to do research. He learned that in the mid 1600's there was the council of Trent, and the church, which was trying to control people, forbid the healing practice by his family; they saw it as a possible threat to their power. "The bishop in nearby Foligno wanted to stop it, so he ex-communicated one of my ancestors," Cancelli explained. The ex-communicated ancestor put a curse on the bishop for stopping him from healing people. The malediction went something like this: "You will fall sick and have to come to me to be healed." And so it happened. The bishop needed help from Cancelli, and Cancelli was soon back in business, so to speak, even though there was never any exchange of money between the healer and his patients. It was always strictly a matter of donations.

In 1840, Pius IX was bishop of Spoleto and often came to Cancelli. Then he became pope and went to live in Rome. He developed a serious case of arthritis and sent two Swiss guards to fetch Giovan Battista Cancelli, who was the carrier of the gift at that time. Cancelli was out cutting wood to make charcoal, and he was dirty from head to toe. He was picked up and put in the pope's carriage; understandably, he was terribly frightened. No one explained to him where he was going or why. He thought that he was being arrested.

To Cancelli's amazement, he was deposited in the Vatican, cleaned, bathed, and taken to the pope. He worked his magic on the pontiff, and then the latter asked him, "What should I do now?" With great simplicity and innocence, Cancelli replied, "Have faith."

The next day, the pope was healed. He granted an audience to an English gentleman who asked for a blessing for his sick wife. The pope referred the request to Cancelli, and the wife was healed. The story spread about Cancelli's gift. Cancelli knew he could travel, but he always had to return to the village to live or the gift would be lost.

How did Maurizio Cancelli find out about this story? "The pope's secretary wrote to the bishop of Foligno saying he should instruct Cancelli in proper Christianity because he had the nerve to tell the pope to have faith! So there was a written record," Cancelli said. He was able to trace his family's tradition back to the 1200's. "It makes me shiver that since that time, there has been no interruption in the lineage. The gift has been passed down, always to a male, father to son."

Cancelli paused again, and reflected that people who live in close contact with nature have higher powers and great insight. This is what made him become a shepherd, and he kept forty-five sheep on the hills of the small village. "My ancestors were simple people," he said. "They had no sophistication but they had contact with nature."

When Cancelli was in his 20's, he was skeptical about the family powers. He reluctantly accompanied his father to see a critically ill man in a faraway village. After a hands-on healing, neither the elder nor the younger Cancelli thought the man would survive. Some time later, they were visiting the same remote village, and they stopped in at the man's house to see if he was still alive. To their astonishment, the man's wife answered the door and said that the day after the healing, her husband had gotten up and gone to work in his fields.

"It was a shock to me, almost like a slap in the face," Cancelli explained. "That was the event that made me drop my skepticism. Now I am committed to remaining here in the village, so the gift of healing is not lost. I am an artist. I have had offers, and I have had doubts, but I was never seriously tempted. Doctors come here for help. Poor people come here for help. This is what I must do."

I longed to experience the healing tradition, and I told Cancelli about something that was bothering me. He led us into a small wooden hut with a simple altar and portraits of the two apostles on the wall. He lit a candle, beckoned me to kneel on a small stool, and then ran his hands lightly over my shoulder, spine, legs, and feet. He intoned a prayer as he did this.

After the healing, Cancelli refused to explain his work or speak any more about it. It was almost as if he was afraid that saying too much would disturb the healing energy. He willingly talked about his wonderfully vivid paintings that were combinations of nature and classical architecture. The architecture seemed logical, but it was as whimsical and impossible as the works of Escher.

In the family tradition, Cancelli offered guests to the village hospitality. He opened a restaurant called "Locando dei due Apostoli" where divine food was served at lunch and dinnertime at very affordable prices. The meal we had included antipasto (with fresh, home-made prosciutto), pasta with truffles, grilled sheep that was raised in Cancelli, rocciata (an Umbrian speciality made of nuts, walnuts, apples, pine nuts, raisins, sugar and bread crumbs), a local liquor called Alchermens, and wine.

The day that we visited with Maurizo Cancelli there were no other visitors in Cancelli. I later read that many people from all over the world found out about the healer and headed to the tiny village for help.

Did I get healed from what troubled me? To tell the truth, I wasn't really ill. I just longed to experience what Cancelli did. And I can report honestly that I felt a vivid vibration from his hands and he said it was the energy that was handed down from the two apostles. Because of their images that were always present when Cancelli healed, I think that what a local man told me may be true: the energy of the two saints was still present because Cancelli kept the family contract with them that was made millennia ago. He stayed in the village, keeping up his side of the bargain, and they kept up theirs: their vibrational energy stayed with him. And since Peter and Paul learned their healing technique from Jesus and transmitted it to Cancelli, it could be said that the energy of Jesus was present, too, when Cancelli performed his healings.

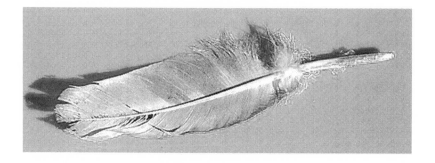

Chapter XI

JERUSALEM SYNDROME, TURKEY, AND SYRIA

My experiences with Rubens Faria, Jr., who manifested Dr. Fritz, and Maurizio Cancelli, who inherited his healing power from two apostles, reaffirmed my feeling that there are great mysteries in the world, inexplicable phenomena, and they cannot be understood through the brain. Rationality, science, and intellect, however, are not incompatible with supranatural occurrences, and the former sometimes find themselves willingly or spontaneously engaged with the latter.

A rare psychosis seems to me to be one of those things that is both explainable and beyond our logical understanding. It takes place in the human mind and body, but may open to other times, realms, and dimensions. It is named after, and takes place in, Jerusalem.

Tourists afflicted with the condition called "Jerusalem Syndrome" have been found wandering in the Judean desert wrapped in hotel bed sheets or camped in front of the Church of the Holy Sepulcher, convinced they will soon be birthing the infant Jesus.

Some years ago, I visited Dr. Bar-El, the "father of Jerusalem Syndrome," at Kfar Shaul Hospital in Jerusalem. The gray-haired doctor looked spookily like Dr. Freud as he leaned back in his chair, puffing on a cigar, with his glasses perched on the tip of his nose. He didn't invent Jerusalem Syndrome, which has been described by foreign visitors over the last few hundred years. But he is the *pater psychosis* who promoted treatment for and research into the illness.

Bar-El explained that there are three categories of tourists who get Jerusalem Syndrome. The first is individual visitors to Israel who were already suffering from mental illness in their countries of origin. They come to Jerusalem with psychotic ideas that they feel they must act upon in the Holy Land. The second group — the largest one— is pilgrims who arrive with deep religious convictions. In some cases, they belong to fringe groups rather than regular churches. They believe they must do specific things to bring about major events like the coming of the Messiah, the appearance of the anti-Christ, the war of Armageddon, or the resurrection of Jesus Christ.

The third group is the "real" Jerusalem Syndrome. It affects completely sane tourists without any psychiatric or drug abuse history. They arrive with normal tour groups and suddenly they develop what Bar-El called a "specific imperative psychotic reaction." In all cases, the same clinical picture emerges. It begins with general anxiety and nervousness and then the tourist feels an imperative need to visit the holy places. First, he undertakes a series of purification rituals like shaving all his body hair, cutting his nails and washing himself over and over before he dons white clothes. Most often, he lifts the white sheets from his hotel room. Then he begins to cry or to sing Biblical or religious songs in a very loud voice.

The next step is an actual visit to the holy places, most often from the life of Jesus. The afflicted tourist begins to deliver a sermon — which is frequently a confused oration — where he exhorts humanity to change their behavior by becoming calmer, purer, and less sophisticated or worldly.

Dr. Bar-El said that from the psychiatric point of view, the most interesting thing is that besides this curious psychotic reaction, the patient doesn't see strange things or hear voices, and he recalls everything that happens. He knows he is John Smith or Will O'Casey, he doesn't lose his own identity, and the illness passes completely in five to seven days. Sometimes, the afflicted visitor is on a package tour of the Mediterranean, which includes Greece, Egypt and Israel. He may be completely sane in Greece, he develops Jerusalem Syndrome in Israel, it passes in five days, and then he continues on with the group to Egypt.

From a religious point of view, the Syndrome seems to favor Protestants, who account for 97 per cent of all cases. Their current religious practices aren't very important; the essential element seems to be an ultra-orthodox upbringing where the Bible was the book of choice for family reading and problem solving. Several theologians who are fascinated by Jerusalem Syndrome speculate that Catholics have intermediaries like the Virgin Mary and saints. They also have other geographical locales that are important to them, like the Vatican, which is presided over by the Pope. But for Protestants, the only personification in the Bible is Jesus Christ, and the Holy Land is the only place where they can go to follow his life. So they are very concentrated on Jesus and this sets the stage for the advent of the strange, temporary Holy Land aberration.

Although the whole problem of Jerusalem Syndrome may seem to us like a benign curiosity, it was taken very seriously in Israel when I was there. Everyone involved in security, tourism, or health and welfare was on the lookout for afflicted visitors. In an average year, about 40 tourists required hospitalization for psychiatric illness. Most were from the first two groups, who had severe problems before they arrived in Israel. A few — perhaps three or four — developed true Jerusalem Syndrome.

Dr. Bar-El took a long puff on his cigar and got down to specifics. He said that a woman was picked up by the police for kicking and hitting people at the Church of the Holy Sepulcher. "I am the Prophetess of the Olive Tree," she proclaimed. "I am very powerful, and I will announce the coming of Christ." She was in a very anxious state, and she insisted she had to remain outdoors, under the influence of the sun and the moon so that her branches could grow green, which was a sign of the immediate return of Jesus. If she was moved inside, under a roof, her branches would grow black, and that would be a sign of the anti-Christ. Besides these claims and her aggressive behavior, everything else about the Olive Tree Prophetess was completely normal.

Another seemingly normal man was a teacher from Denmark. Every year he went to Jerusalem, because only there could he dialogue with the Virgin Mary. Lourdes and other miraculous sites didn't do it for him.

Bar-El talked about a memorable case, which actually led to one of the first instances of collaboration between Palestinian and Israeli police. The Palestinians found a man without clothes, money or ID, and after interrogation they figured out he wasn't a security risk. They had no idea what to do with him, so they contacted an Israeli officer. The Israeli asked only one question: "Is the guy really completely nude?" "No," answered the Palestinian," he is wearing an animal skin." "Oh," said the Israeli, "you've got another John the Baptist." It was the sixth John the Baptist the Israelis had run into.

John the Baptists usually did days of purification between Jerusalem and the Galilee before ending up at the Jordan River to baptize Jesus or the first Christians…and part of the trek was through Palestinian territory.

Over the years, I have asked a few psychiatrists, imams, rabbis, and priests, what they thought about Jerusalem Syndrome. Most hadn't heard of it. Others just dismissed it as a bizarre, temporary mental illness. But two expressed different opinions. The first said, "Who knows? It could be a case of reincarnation." And the second said, "Energy is neither created nor destroyed. When we die, the energy released goes somewhere. We are not sure where. It can go to different places, not just one place. Maybe for a moment in time people with Jerusalem Syndrome actually have a glimpse of when part of their energy was contained in the Biblical figure." When I commented that multiple people thought they were the same Biblical figure, he said, "Energy doesn't stay in one lump. It scatters. So a lot of people could have been separate parts of a person who lived long ago. Numerous people think they are Cleopatra, or Caesar, or a Medieval Saint, you know."

I asked if he was kidding and he said, "Life is a great mystery. Many things happen that we cannot explain. I stopped laughing at them a long time ago."

One priest who I met in a church in Tunis told me he had a very strange experience when he went to Damascus, Syria. He was visiting the underground stone church that is said to contain the remains of the house of Saint Ananais. It was there that Saul, who had previously been a brutal persecutor of the followers of Jesus, went after he had a conversion experience on the road to Damascus that left him blind. Ananais restored his sight, and baptized him.

The priest said he became Saul. "First I felt that I was Saul," the priest began. "I sensed that I couldn't see. There was a blinding light and it obscured my vision. Then nothing was clear and it was like there was a film over my eyes. I fell to my knees at the feet of Ananais. He said words to me, but I don't remember what they were. He put his hands on me. I started to shake, both inside and out. It was completely real to me. Not like a dream, but as though I really was Saul. And Ananais was with me. My hair was wet from the baptism. And then I saw a light again, and I was no longer Saul. I became Paul the Apostle. Was it a past life experience? I have wondered that. I don't know. Maybe I will never know. Was it a mini Jerusalem Syndrome? It certainly happened to me, and even as I speak about it I can feel it."

A few years later, Paul and I traveled throughout Syria, where people were extremely hospitable and the antiquities were the best we had ever seen. We decided that we would visit the alleged home of Saint Ananais in Damascus, where Saul was healed and baptized. The simple underground stone church, which had an early Christian origin, was suffused with an extremely holy aura. Although there were plain wooden benches, one woman rocked back and forth as she prayed on her knees on the floor. The few other visitors besides us stood silently, with their heads bowed.

And when we were in eastern Turkey, we visited the stone ruins of the home of Saul in Tarsus. I recall seeing part of the foundations, and an ancient well. Restoration of the Roman street nearby was in progress, and our guide told us that Saul came from a very observant Jewish family who were fairly wealthy. Apparently, they could afford to send him to Jerusalem for education, because a sign indicated that Saul had studied there with Rabbi Gamaliel.

It always moved me when I visited a site associated with a figure in the Bible or in history. They were real people, not just literary creations. Saul had a family. They shopped on a nearby street. He drank water from a well. He studied in Jerusalem. He underwent a conversion. Was it possible that the priest who told me about his visit to Ananais's home in Damascus was having an authentic reincarnation experience? There is no way for him, or for us, to know. We can believe or disbelieve it, because ultimately it is a question of belief. There is no way for our rational minds to know.

When I told a Catholic friend about the priest and his experience from another lifetime, he smiled and said, "If you want an experience with the dead coming back, check out Day of the Dead."

I smiled back at him. It was already on my radar.

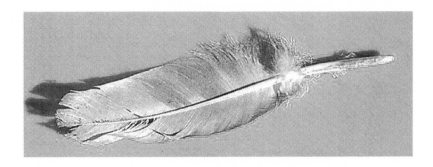

Chapter XII.

DAYS OF THE DEAD
IN MEXICO

When I lived in Los Angeles, I was introduced to Day of the Dead celebrations downtown on Olvera Street, but hardly registered the importance they had in Mexican culture. I thought it was vaguely spooky that people bought sweets that looked like skulls, hung paper cutouts in the shape of skeletons, and had tattoos of skulls and bones on their arms.

Then, some years ago, Paul and I were visiting Taos, New Mexico, and we wandered into Starr Interiors, the gallery owned by Susanna Starr. The high-quality textiles that had been created by indigenous Zapotec weavers in Mexico captivated us. The handmade rugs and wall hangings ranged from pre-Columbian motifs to pictorials to elegant contemporary designs and Southwestern-style pillows. Susy, as we came to know her, told us about her multi-decade-long association with the Zapotec weavers, and their history in the Oaxaca valley, dating back to the fifth century B.C.E.

Over the next months, we became very friendly with Susy and her *compañero* John, and Susy suggested that Paul and I make a film about the weavers and go to Oaxaca, Mexico as a foursome.

We left for Mexico on a day when the golden leaves of the aspen trees were fluttering to the earth in the mountains above Santa Fe, and Mexico was preparing for the Day of The Dead festivities. In Mexico, the Day of the Dead is a national holiday, in deference to the indigenous populations all over the country.

Because of Susy's relationships, we were invited to stay in the home of a family of Zapotec weavers in the small, traditional village of Teotitlan del Valle in the Oaxaca Valley that was founded in the 15th century. And what we knew as one-day Day of the Dead turned out to be a cycle of events.

The family altar was lovingly and artistically arranged with flowers (especially golden marigolds), candles, photos of the deceased, and their favorite foods when they were alive. A smaller altar was for the children who had died; besides sugar skulls, it had some of the children's little toys. The smells, tastes, and photos were placed to entice the *difuntos* (departed ones) to come back for a visit. It was the time of year when the dead and the living celebrated together, and the deceased could hear stories about themselves and prayers for their spirits, and see how much their families and friends loved and remembered them.

The day before the celebrations started, Paul and I strolled first to the church and then the cemetery, and what we saw was unusual and arresting. A small family carried large, multi-hued flowers and watched silently as two gravediggers dug a hole and exhumed the ancestral bones that were buried in their family gravesite. Then they lowered the shrouded body of a recently deceased family member into the same hole, added the exhumed bones on top of him, and covered them all with earth. As the body of the newly deceased person decomposed, it would mix with and become part of the ancestors.

When the gravediggers explained to us what they had done, I found it deeply moving. Not only do the living relate to the dead, but the dead relate to, and are mingled with those who died before them. The continuity of ancestry is palpable, physical, and it takes place below the earth, in the dark, rich soil that nourishes them and us.

Later, after we visited the impressive and important Zapotec pre-Colombian ruins of Monte Alban, we were walking back to our car and we saw a small cemetery. We made a slight detour, and saw two indigenous gravediggers. We knew exactly what they were doing as they mingled the bones of the departed. We wondered if this was a tradition that went back thousands of years, as Monte Alban was one of the earliest cities of Mesoamerica. The gravediggers said they thought it was very possible.

That evening we returned to the village, and saw that the family whose house we were staying in had added more food and flowers to the colorful *ofrenda* (altar).

The next day, which was the first day of the *Dia de Muertos* cycle, village church bells tolled to welcome back the children who had died. Some families went to the cemetery with fruit and candy and *calaveras* (skulls) and laid it all at the graves of the "little angels" as one woman called them. She prayed for the soul of her young niece who had died.

That evening, we went to visit another family of weavers, and the mother made spicy hot chocolate for us, and whipped up a froth with an ornately carved wooden *molinillo (*whisk or blender), which she rolled between her hands. She handed us the deliciously aromatic drink with smiling hospitality.

The next day, the adult *difuntos* came back. The family we were staying with decorated the graves of their deceased family members, leaving *pan de muerto* (sweet rolls), orange marigolds, mescal, fruits, nuts, and incense. The entire cemetery was decorated with cardboard skeletons, brightly colored tissue paper decorations, and the favorite foods of the departed, which could be washed down with beer, soda, and *atole* (a cornmeal drink), as well as bottles of mescal and tequila.

A young woman explained to us that the dead eat the spiritual essence of the food, but another, older woman corrected her and said they actually eat the food and enjoy it. It may not seem like the food has been eaten, because they have a different kind of appetite.

That evening, it was party time, and it was a raucous, joyous event shared by the living and the dead. Mariachis, including some whose trumpets sounded a little off-key from being tipsy, rocked the cemetery. Young men strolled around jauntily, dressed as black-and-white skeletons. Locals were adorned in brightly colored, embroidered textiles, and the smell of *copal* incense permeated the air. It wasn't just a party because of course there was sadness for those who had died recently. It was an honoring and celebration of the lives of those who had passed.

The party, we heard, went on all night. Then, when it was over, the dead departed for another year, after which they would come back again.

A few years ago, anxious to return to Mexico for the *Dia de Muertos*, we took a group of student travel writers and photographers to study and learn at a magnificent 500-year-old hacienda in Guanajuato state. Every morning and night we held classes, and every day we traveled around, exploring the rich culture and history of the area. We told the students very little about what to expect, so they would experience it all for themselves, and form their own impressions.

On November 2nd, the cemetery in the town of Dolores Hidalgo was ablaze with aubergine-and-sunburst-hued marigolds and mums that were carried by friends and family members of the departed, and placed lovingly at their gravesites. At one tomb, mariachis sang and strummed their best tunes. Farther on, there was a big band sound, with trombones pumping out tunes for the dead. Elsewhere, shoulders swayed to music. And one grave was adorned with a *serape* and an oversized *sombrero*: visitors were invited to adorn themselves with the clothes and take selfies.

All good parties involve food, and visitors to the cemetery brought ample picnics and laid out the favorite foods and imbibables of the departed. Some talked to the dead, or read them their favorite poems. The living prayed for the dead, and several people told our enthralled students that the souls of the dead are attracted by the offerings, and their presence can be felt. "I certainly feel them!" one of our students exclaimed.

In the city of Guanajuato, talented makeup artists adorned young women with arresting whiteface, garish eye makeup, and blood-red lips. The women then donned long, flowing skirts, heels, and broad-brimmed hats, and became the *Katrinas*, the images of death, as they paraded through the streets in skeletal splendor in time to the drummers who accompanied them. "No wonder the souls of the dead are attracted; it's one helluva party!" one of our students said as she danced in place and munched on a *pan de muertos*.

In San Miguel de Allende, arty altars made from flowers and legumes lined the streets around the *jardin* (central garden). They paid tribute to the departed, and fascinated the living. Locals and visitors wore face paint, ate *pan de muertos* and sugary *calaveras* that were sold everywhere, and music blared from loud speakers. Apparently oblivious to the music, an English-speaking woman recited a poem, written in doggerel, that she had written for her deceased mother. It was full of insider jokes about their life together and her mother's obsession with fashion, ironing, cleaning house, and having a mirror or two in every room.

I stood at the edge of the jardin, reflecting that we cannot prevent death from coming to all of us. But maybe the Mexican Day of the Dead is a way to get the last laugh at that relentless guy with the scythe. Death can take the body, but the soul lives on in the hearts of those who remain behind.

"Loss is sad, missing someone is painful, but around the Day of the Dead, the departed are honored, prayed for, and even amused with funny stories and objects from their lives," a young Mexican man told me. "Do you think they hear you?" I asked. He looked at me, blinked, and looked again, as though he couldn't comprehend the question. "Do you think the dead hear what you are saying?" I asked again. "Of course they do! They hear everything. I bet they even hear what we're thinking!" he exulted. Then he smiled and confided, "My abuelo (grandfather), who died nine years ago, even said he is going to find a beloved for me. He'll be dancing at my wedding." Then, after a pause, he added, "Of course he was just answering me because I asked him to help. You have to ask, you know."

Recently, I was in Campeche, Mexico, in Yucatan. "Have you heard about Pomuch?" Luis asked me. Luis, who works in a hotel in Campeche, Mexico, is a compendium of all things Maya. "No," I answered.

"Once a year, for the Day of the Dead, the Maya who live there clean the bones of their ancestors."

I was careful about how I phrased my question.

"You mean the bones of the dead are...actually...dug up and cared for?"

"Yes. Their families wait a number of years until the bodies have decomposed, of course. And then they clean them in the cemetery."

It took me exactly two days to find my way to the cemetery in Pomuch. Arturo, who owns Xtampak Tours in Campeche and is of

Maya heritage, volunteered to drive me. It was a sizzling February day under a merciless sun, but oblivious to the heat I bounded out of Arturo's car. Without a word, he entered the cemetery and beckoned me to join him.

I followed him down a row lined on both sides by brightly colored, stacked, open niches with the names of the deceased hand-painted on the outside. Wilberth Canche Coox, Maria Isabel Euan Pech, Jose Maria Chan.

I peered into the niches, and saw small, open boxes filled with the bones Luis had described. Skulls, long bones, brown hair, teeth, even a rib cage. The bones were so white they looked as though they had been impeccably bleached.

Eneyda D. Calle Cauich. Sr. Alfonhso Chan Axe. Sra Victoria Canche Cohuo. Maria Guadalujpe Poot Tuz. Hermila Haas Kantun.

"It's like they're alive," I whispered to Arturo. Although Luis had told me about it, I was unprepared for how affecting it was to walk by each ancestor, and see how lovingly the insides of the niches were prepared and arranged, with embroidered cloths and flowers.

"The Maya don't believe in death," Arturo said matter-of-factly. "For them, their ancestors are still alive and they come to the cemetery to speak to them, keep them up to date. They come here to visit their parents and grandparents when they need to talk or are having problems. It gives them solace and guidance."

Arturo wiped the sweat that cascaded down his forehead and continued. "For the Maya, deceased family members are living in another dimension. The *inframundo.* The underworld. But they are still alive in the underworld. That's why the families come to visit them. You talk to them like they are alive because they *are* alive," Arturo says.

81

My mind flashed back to what I had learned in school about the conservation of mass. It had been widely accepted since the 18th century. Matter cannot be created or destroyed. Anything made up of atoms, including humans, can be rearranged in space, or changed in form. Transformation. It was what Arturo was talking about. The dead existed in another form, another dimension.

I walked slowly down each row of the cemetery, pondering Arturo's words. The dead still exist. They are alive. Their families communicate with them. A young woman entered the cemetery, and set down her nylon bags filled with groceries. She had come to speak to her mother, perhaps, or maybe an aunt or her grandparents. It was a normal part of her daily life.

"This is very ancient, thousands of years old," Arturo said. "The Maya had special burial areas for their dead. From October fifteenth until November first every year, the women do the cleaning of the bones. It is not a sad thing. It is a celebration – like you are preparing the deceased for a party. The priest comes to make a ceremony on November first for the children who died, and on November second for the adults. And every year the bones are cleaned."

Arturo smiled. "The Maya love their dead, you know," he said. "They're dead, but they're still alive."

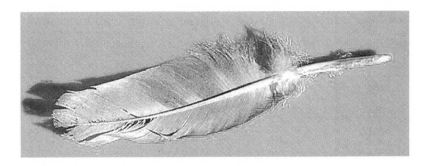

Chapter XIII.

TOMBS OF THE RABBIS IN ISRAEL

It was oddly familiar. If I hadn't talked to the young Mexican man about his deceased matchmaking *abuelo* or been to the festival of the Ghriba on Djerba island in Tunisia, I probably would have rolled my eyes with incredulity. I was in Israel, and an Israeli kindergarten teacher, who seemed sane and intelligent, looked me in the eyes as she explained how she met her husband. "I was forty years old, and I was just about to give up on meeting a mate. Then I prayed at the tomb of Jonathan ben Uziel, and two weeks later I met him. Eight months later we were married."

I chalked it up to coincidence until I met an Israeli artist who was bubbly, upbeat and also very credible. "My life has changed," she said. "I was so lonely but then I prayed at the tomb of Jonathan ben Uziel and met my soul mate."

I was visiting Safed, in the north of Israel, in the vicinity of the tomb, and decided to check out the departed matchmaker. Armed with a healthy dose of skepticism, I entered the women's side of the low, whitewashed building, called a *tsyun*, that is made of local rocks, cement, earth and stones, and which houses the remains of the famed first century C.E. rabbi.

Inside, the sepulcher was draped in a dark velvet cloth. Women prayed earnestly from Hebrew prayer books and several deposited coins and bills into charity tins. I looked around the room at the prayer offerings women had left behind: brightly colored cloth, silk and chiffon scarves, plastic hair ornaments and underpants. Underpants?!

"This is where legendary rabbis inspired the Hebrew people thousands of years ago. It is also where, in the medieval period, brilliant rabbis developed and disseminated the mystical Torah studies known as Kaballah," our guide Nurit told us.

The hills around Safed are dotted with ancient tombs. To Jewish believers, these tombs of long-deceased *tsaddikim* (holy men) are the meeting place between the living and the dead. People make pilgrimages to the burial places to ask for blessings, favors, surcease from suffering.

"They do not actually pray to the ancient rabbis; rather, they pray that the departed *tsaddikim* will intercede on their behalf with God," Nurit explained. "And because God looks favorably upon holy men and the merit of their lives, he is more likely to grant a request." "Nurit, why do women leave underpants at the tomb of a rabbi?" I asked. "Maybe it's because it's something very close to their reproductive organs and they want to get pregnant. Perhaps it's because underpants are very personal. Actually, you'd have to ask one of the women who left them."

I decided to visit one other grave in the small, ancient village of Meron — perched on the side of Mount Meron, with its abundant greenery, trees and views of Safed and the Galilee. Meron village is the resting place of Shimon bar Yochai. One of the most famous of the *tsaddikim*, he is credited with being the author of the central book of Kaballah, called the Zohar, almost two thousand years ago. Believers go there to pray for prosperity, peace in their souls, fertility and healing.

Paul and I climbed up the narrow main street of Meron to two stone archways with Hebrew inscriptions (one arch for men and one for women) that led to the whitewashed *tzyun*. Paul entered the men's section, looked around, shot a few photos, shrugged and exited.

"Don't ask. Nothing happened," he reported. "Nothing."

But for me, on the women's side, something very different and highly unexpected was going on. As soon as I entered the room, my body began to shake and I started to cry. I looked around, self-consciously. A few women sat on benches, and others stood facing the walls or the tomb itself, praying. No one was paying any attention to me as tears splattered the front of my pale blue shirt. I walked, no, I wove my way to the tomb, placed my head on the cool, white exterior, and prayed and asked for help with a very difficult situation I was going through. I felt as though — how can I describe this? — as though my words were heard.

When I came out into the stark afternoon sun, Paul was waiting for me. I had been gone about twenty minutes. I told him what had happened, and he listened. He was surprised but couldn't really connect to what I was describing. "A dead rabbi heard your words?" he asked. "Okay, honey, if you say so."

Our next stop was at the tomb of Baba Sali in Netivot. Baba Sali was a Moroccan holy man who is credited with many miraculous healings. He died in 1984 and has a very large following in North Africa and Israel. I was turned off as soon as I arrived at the large and well-developed site with its multiple buildings because it felt very institutionalized. A well-dressed male employee spoke to visitors, droning on and on about buildings and books and the history of the place. When I looked up, a bus arrived, and a line of Yemenite women got out. I was immediately drawn to them, and started to talk to them in English, broken Hebrew, French and hand-signals. One of them, an older woman dressed in black, grabbed my hand, and I followed her. She took me to a small booth where a man sold boxes of candles. I did as she did, and purchased one, for about two dollars. Then she led me to a large outdoor furnace, where a fire was burning. One by one, she removed each of the 12 candles from the box. "Each one is a family member or good friend," she explained as she tossed each of them into the fire. "I pray for them." "Now you, now you," she urged.

I did as she did — asking for healing for a sick family member, romance for friends, general well being for people I care about. Then she headed into one of the rooms and announced, reverently, "Baba Sali." She placed her hands on a tomb and began to pray. I just watched her. Several of the other Yemenite women joined her, and did the same thing. They prayed aloud, fervently, obviously in a state of great devotion.

A small group of tourists arrived in the room and their guide began to speak in English about the tomb." This is where the architect who built the Baba Sali center is buried," the guide explained.

I felt terrible for my new Yemenite friend. She was praying at the wrong tomb! I decided to tell her this wasn't where her beloved Baba Sali was interred, so that she could re-direct her prayers. To my surprise, the news didn't disturb her or her friends at all. "If this was the Baba Sali architect, or someone else, it doesn't matter," said one of them.

It was a person associated with Baba Sali, and that was good enough for them. They continued to pray, and then they moved on to the actual tomb of Baba Sali, and prayed once more. At each spot, they wept and intoned until it was time for them to board the bus again. When my new friend hugged me good-bye, she put her hand over her heart and sighed. "Good, good," she said. It was clear that she had gotten from Baba Sali what she came for.

I began to ask Israelis I met about other tombs, and they all said that the major annual tomb event would be taking place in a few days at the gravesite of Shimon bar Yochai. It was important to go there before sunset. Great. I already knew where it was. I would go back there again. Paul agreed without much enthusiasm. I suppose he chalked it up as the price he had to pay for being married to me.

And so, on the holiday of Lag B'Omer , in the merry month of May, we headed to Meron. Lag B'Omer , which I had experienced at the Ghriba synagogue in Tunisia, is a spring holiday that is associated with bringing barley offerings to the ancient Temple in Jerusalem, more than two millennia ago. Over the centuries, several tragic events happened at this time of year, and it is a period of semi-mourning for observant Jews. But on Lag B'Omer , there was a break from suffering, miracles occurred, and the day is happy and celebratory. I had experienced that joy on Djerba island.

When we arrived at Meron, the place was unrecognizable. Pilgrims had to park 10 or even 20 minutes away because the roads were jammed with cars. The streets of the town were bursting with women, children, and bearded men attired in traditional, orthodox black clothing: well over a hundred thousand believers came from all over Israel to pay homage to Shimon bar Yochai, on the anniversary of his death.

"He was the most joyous of the rabbis, and on his deathbed he revealed the light of the Torah to his students. He asked that his death be marked with festivity," an Orthodox rabbi named Mendy explained to us.

It was clear that Shimon bar Yochai's devotees followed his wishes, and they arrived in a state of celebratory exuberance.

On the main street, it was like a carnival. In makeshift booths, vendors sold crafts, religious objects, clothes, books, dates, nuts, and soft drinks. Families were camped out in tents. Men in long beards asked for charity or offered blessings.

"According to tradition, if a man and woman are having fertility problems, the man gives out the contents of 18 bottles of wine on Lag B'Omer to cure the barrenness," the local rabbi who was our guide informed us.

The number 18 is favorable in Judaism, and it is associated with life and living. The origin of this belief seems to come from the two Hebrew letters — *chet* and *yud* — that form the word "*chai*," which means life. In Gematria or numerology, *chet* equals eight and yud is 10. If you add them up, you get 18.

As Paul and I walked through the street, young men pressed glasses of wine on us; we drank, of course, because we knew they were trying to dispense the contents of 18 bottles and it would be rude not to honor their desire for children.

As we advanced toward the tomb, music with Hebrew lyrics was blasting from loud speakers. On huge screens, there was a video of the much-admired Lubavitcher Rabbi, and in the street, people gave out fliers and prayer cards bearing the name of Nachman of Bratslav, the famed rabbi whose tomb I had visited in Uman, Ukraine. People were hawking wares and hanging out. Were Jews celebrating like Mexicans on the Day of the Dead?

The sun was going down in the west, and as soon as it disappeared, a great bonfire was prepared near the tomb of Shimon bar Yochai. I asked a woman who was standing next to me about the significance of the bonfire. "When Rabbi Shimon revealed the Torah on his deathbed, there was a blazing light around him, and everyone saw it. To this day, he is associated with light, and fires are lit in his honor," she explained.

It was very difficult to see what was going on because of the thousands and thousands of people gathered near the sepulcher. Paul held his camera over his head, clicking away. A rabbi poured olive oil and the bonfire blazed—marking the formal beginning of the festivities. Immediately, there was an eruption of ecstasy. Men in black began to dance and sing with great fervor. Everyone was clapping and stomping and hooting with glee. Men wrapped their prayer shawls and fringed undergarments around each other, and they began to dance, bonded and transported with merriment. Women danced in a circle. Everyone shared food, drinks, and blessings.

The actual tomb was mobbed because, by tradition, men bring their young sons to get their first haircuts on this night. There were no women allowed, but Paul decided to elbow his way in so that he could get some photos. It took him about five minutes to work his way through the crowd. I expected him to stay for a minute or two and re-emerge, but he didn't come out. Half an hour passed, and suddenly I saw Paul. His face was flushed.

"What happened?" I asked, afraid he had had a bad experience. "I got pulled into the dancing," he answered. "I was going to drop out, but I figured maybe I should just go with the experience. I had no idea what I was doing. I just followed what the others did. I put my hands around the shoulders of the men next to me, and I kicked up heels, just as they did. There were dozens and dozens of men in the dance."

"Did you enjoy it?" I asked. "Enjoy?" "Yes. Was it fun?'

Paul grew very quiet. "It took me by surprise," he said. "It wasn't really about fun. I found it oddly bonding, moving and meaningful. It wasn't something cerebral. I could almost feel the presence of the dead rabbi."

"Okay, honey, if you say so," I said with a wink.

So in Meron, I thought I had been heard and Paul felt the presence of someone dead for 2,000 years.

Were we imagining it? I don't think so. Is it really that easy for the living to access the deceased? If both parties are willing, I believe the answer is yes.

Chapter XIV.

THE YAMABUSHI
IN JAPAN

Recently, Paul and I received a highly unusual invitation to undergo private training with the Yamabushi master in the remote mountains of Shonai, Japan. The monks had seen a TEDx talk I did about Deep Travel, and thought we were a good match. I knew nothing about the Yamabushi monks because I like to travel without preconceptions, and in this case it's a good thing I didn't know anything until a few nights before our departure, because I might have canceled the trip out of fear. Make that panic.

An email informed us that Shonai was one of the snowiest places on earth, and this year the snows came even earlier than usual. The pilgrims' lodge where we were going to stay had no heat, but they would bring in a few kerosene heaters. We had to sit on the cold floor a lot of the time. The toilets were in a separate building, which meant going outside, and, like the corridors of the lodge, it had no heat. We would have to meditate under a frigid waterfall, and sit in a room with smoke from chili peppers to test our endurance. For the entire multi-day training, we couldn't brush our teeth and Paul couldn't shave. We could only speak one word, which I couldn't remember no matter how hard I tried, even though I think I have a certain facility with languages. And the worst was this: to hike up to just one of the shrines we had to climb 2,000 steps, in the snow and ice, mind you, and I had shredded my meniscus by falling off an electric bike and I couldn't climb 10 steps. Forget sitting in lotus position.

It turns out that the Yamabushi monks were once numerous and had considerable political power. They were fearsome warriors, religious ascetics, and had a reputation for being able to control the weather. Most Japanese people think the Yamabushi disappeared after the Meiji Restoration of 1868 when the government was restructured and the new constitution resulted in the destruction of the warrior classes, which included the Samurai and the Yamabushi. But the Yamabushi didn't vanish. They have kept up their secret practices for 1500 years.

Recently, the Master in Shonai decided that people were struggling with stress, and disconnected both from nature and their own true nature. Instead of living in hermetic and ascetic isolation, he began to reach out. People came from all over Japan, eager for the opportunity. Then it was determined that since a few of the monks spoke English, it could be offered to Westerners. We were the first to experience it, with the understanding that we could write about it and photograph parts of it. Usually the training takes place in the summer, or the warmer months, but we agreed to go in the deep winter.

It was a two-hour flight (or four-hour train ride) from Tokyo to Shonai, and we were met by several monks and driven to Dewa Sanzan, the holy mountains. We arrived at a tall, open gate, which we learned separated the mundane from the sacred. Behind it was Daishōbō, Master Hoshino's pilgrims' retreat. As we walked towards it, our breath froze and I half expected our words to crack, like icicles, and crash to the ground.

We met Master Hoshino, who looked like a cross between Santa Claus and a snow owl. He was sitting at a low table, on a *tatami* mat. He took out a small wooden piece, which Tak, our monk translator, said was a household memorial to his deceased mother. Master Hoshino went on to say that our training would be a spiritual death and rebirth. We would dress in white, the traditional color for funerals. The clothes we were handed were so complicated to put on, with ties and pantaloons and wrapping and lacing and a head cover, that, for the entire training, Tak had to dress me as though I were a toddler.

To my great relief, and, truth be told, in answer to my prayers, there was a snowstorm, so our training took place inside the lodge. No meditating under a frozen waterfall and, no climbing 2,000 steps that were probably coated in ice, which was hidden by snow.

The lodge is nestled in the midst of the three sacred mountains of Dewa Sanzan: Mount Haguro, which represents the present; Mount Gassan, which embodies the past; and Mount Yaduno, which stands for the future. "After death, the spirit stays at the lower level of the mountains before progressing up to the higher ones," the Master said. "During the training, you will become silent ghosts. In walking the sacred mountains, we are born again, and we come to our senses."

Yamabushi, which is unique to Japan, is a blending of Esoteric Buddhism, Shintoism, and an animistic spirituality that goes back to the roots of Japanese culture and identity. "Nature is the teacher," Hoshino told us, through Tak.

We were given a simple meal of miso soup, pickled vegetables, and a bowl of boiled rice. We were instructed to eat "like hungry ghosts in hell." I'm a pretty fast eater, but I was still gulping down my first vegetables when Hoshino had finished his entire bowl. It probably took me two minutes to eat, but I think I understood that we were not supposed to linger over our food or have all the pleasures of taste that we enjoy in life. The goal of the intense meditation and prayers, the orders barked with the required one-word answer (which, alas, I continued not to remember), and the harsh physical training, was to stop our thinking minds, which separate us from nature. We had to die to an old way of being — thinking-led —and learn to trust our feelings and take emotional risks that could expand our lives and open us up to the natural world around us. By experiencing a death, we would walk the path of inner peace and self-awareness.

The last day, it was announced that we would be ascending Mt. Haguro. I went into instant panic mode about those steps, but, happily, Hoshino drove us the back way. We walked in his snowy, waist-deep footprints to several small shrines where the Master bowed, blew his conch shell trumpet, clapped and prayed. Then we performed ritual hand washing. Finally we walked through a red *tori* gate and entered Sanjin Gosaiden, the main shrine. Two Shinto Priests, attired in green and purple robes with gold designs, greeted and blessed Hoshino, and performed a ceremony for which we were given no explanation.

When we exited the shrine, I was about to sink low into my winter jacket to brace against the cold, but I felt no cold. I also felt no heat, no wind, no air. I heard no noise, and wasn't aware of my body of all. I look around me and saw the most magnificent snow- crested trees. And in a flash, I became one with them.

I understood, without words, what it meant to die. I became one with nature. And as I stood there, I could hear the language of the trees around me. It was like the time, all those years ago, when my father first spoke to me at the cemetery where he is buried. But this time, it was nature speaking. I stood still and listened.

First I heard that I was on the right path. Then I heard words to the effect that all the rituals that took place in the pilgrims' lodge with Master Hoshino were human-made. "The real teacher is the trees."

We returned to the lodge in Hoshino's car, and of course we didn't speak because we had agreed not to. We took off our hats, coats, scarves, boots, and gloves, and walked into the main room. Minutes after we arrived, Hoshino blew his conch shell and Tak announced that the training was over.

"Noooooo!" I called out.

I saw Hoshino's face drop, and Tak looked upset. There was a moment of general confusion, during which I asked Tak what was wrong. He said Master Hoshino was upset that I was disappointed in the training.

"Disappointed? Why would he think that? This is one of the most important things I have done in my life!"

"Master thinks you said 'noooo', and were unhappy it was over because we didn't give you enough and you weren't satisfied," Tak reported.

I stumbled over my words. "Tak, Tak, please, this must be a cultural misunderstanding. I said 'no' because I didn't want it to end. I wanted it to go on and on because it was so powerful."

I watched anxiously as Tak translated for Hoshino, who smiled and nodded. Then, in a moment of shared humor, Hoshino, Tak, Paul, and I all called out "nooooooo." And then we laughed. Hoshino also apologized for his gruff behavior for the previous few days; he explained that was part of the training. We assured him we understood.

And then I asked, in a very calm voice, speaking very slowly, if it was okay for me to tell Master what had happened to me outside of the shrine, in the snow.

Master nodded several times, yes.

I said that suddenly I had understood the language of trees.

"What did the trees say?" Hoshino asked.

"Well...forgive me, Master Hoshino, but they said that all the rituals we did in our Yambushi training are man-made. The real teachers are the trees."

Master smiled, a broad, deep, satisfied smile. "You are a Yamabushi," he said to me. "What the trees said is true. They are the real teachers."

"What elegant humility," I thought. "The Master defers to trees."

When I walked outside for the mundane task of going to the bathroom building, I suddenly noticed trees, bushes, and rocks I hadn't seen before. For a brief moment, I felt like I was one of the ancestors who had once walked the earth, and were now part of the eternal spirit world and I was also part of the nature that surrounded me. I was in the present, past, and future all at the same time. I was dead, I hadn't been born yet, and I was also still myself. It wasn't only that I could understand the trees, but also the snow, the rocks, the bushes. There was no outside of me and no inside of me. It was all the same, all connected and harmonious, without separation or boundaries. I was oblivious to the cold and had no idea of how long my being freed from the shackles of time lasted. After some indeterminate period, which could have been seconds or minutes, I plunked down into myself and continued walking.

I'd had mystical experiences before but I had never had them with nature. I had, at other times, been lifted out of myself into wondrous realms where I was connected to other people, places, and times. I had connected with the living and the dead. But if I hadn't come to Japan and studied with Master Hoshino, I would not have experienced what it was like to be a tree, a stone, or the falling snow. When I returned to the pilgrims' lodge and saw Master I placed my hands in prayer pose and bowed my head slightly. "Sister!" he said. "Brother!" I replied.

When I arrived back home in Santa Fe, I was unable to speak about what happened to me in Japan for months. It required too much effort to try to frame it so that I could describe it, and I was afraid I would vitiate it by talking about it in detail.

As I write these words, it is the first time I have told the whole story. On many occasions, in the past, I listened to indigenous folk tales about a time when humans could communicate with animals, birds, plants, stones, and trees. I have heard indigenous people talk about time being circular and non-linear. They said there are no such things as past, present and future. All time is now. Everything is happening now, even though we perceive it as the past or the future. Time, as we know it, is a rational, logical sequence of events. We know what we did two days ago, a month ago, a year or decade ago. We remember being in a crib or our first day of school. We have vivid recollections of a time when we wandered off in a store and got separated from our mothers. Or a terrifying time when we fell out of a boat and almost drowned. When we recall them, it's as clear and present as though it just happened. Time collapses, and we sometimes feel the powerful emotions as though they are actually taking place now. We know that they aren't occurring in the present, but then why do they feel as if they are?

In many ways, our whole notion of time is something our rational human minds have constructed. We humans have a shared reality of how time passes, and we all agree upon it and synchronize it with calendars, watches, and clocks. But in truth, it doesn't progress in a linear fashion the way we think it does. It is circular. The indigenous people I met were right; everyone who ever lived is here now, but in a different from. They are energetically present. Energy is neither created nor destroyed. It is here and has always been here. It will always be here. The dead and the living co-exist. We will always be here, even when we are gone. Our essence, our energy, will live on. How will we be here? That is the great mystery of what happens after death.

Of course we can interact with the dead; their bodies are gone, but they can also be present if we need them or they need us. Sometimes we invite them to come, and other times they show up spontaneously.

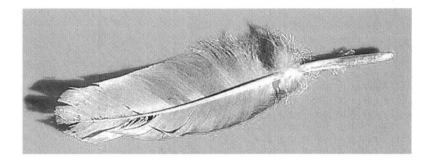

Chapter XV.

TAHITI AND HER ISLANDS

We had checked into a hotel in Tahiti, and the woman behind the desk said, "Teve will take your luggage to your room." Then she whispered, "He's a very famous traditional dancer." I was busy picking up my bag from the desk, shoving the room key into my wallet, and it took me a minute to actually turn around and look at Teve. When I did, my mouth fell open. Teve's entire body was covered with tattoos, both front and back.

Over the next few days, I talked to Teve every chance I got, and I learned that he comes from a royal family on his mother's side, and the tattoos are a way to preserve the story of the chiefs in his lineage. In other words, Teve has a constant reminder of his ancestors; he wears them on his body. He carries them with him in his everyday life.

The story about how he got his tattoos reveals how significant they are to him. He decided that he wanted his tattoos done traditionally, by hand, using a very finely sharpened pig tusk for a needle. It was no longer done in Tahiti, so he went, with two people to support and help him, to Western Samoa. The Samoans, who only do half-body tattoos, were surprised that Teve wanted the tribal art to cover his entire body. They considered him so brave that when he finished he was made a chief orator in Samoa.

It took six weeks to complete Teve's tattooing. He developed an infection, ran a fever every day, bled profusely, and his right calf became very swollen. He battled fear, pain, and physical danger to accomplish his goal, but the result was that he preserved and honored his lineage. It was that important to him.

Two day after our arrival in Tahiti, it was our privilege to meet the very open hearted Minister of Culture of Tahiti. He explained that an ancestor is transformed into an animal, and his ancestor became a shark, which is a protector. For this reason, he wears a tattoo of a shark. Like Teve, the Minister carries his deceased ancestor with him wherever he goes, and he feels connected and protected.

Soon after we arrived, we were very lucky to meet Matarii and Teiva of VIP tours. They took us on a private excursion into the deep culture of Tahiti— and believe me, it is all there, right under the surface. At the Grotto of Maraa, which tourists visit, admire the fresh water lake and the water dripping from the cave walls, and leave, Teiva and Matarii lingered. They told us that the spirits of the dead on the other side of the island fly from the mountain to the waterfall for purification. Then they proceed to a site whose real name means "spirit of the evening," and, lastly, arrive at their final resting place on the island of Raiatea, which is where the roots of Polynesia came from. This cradle of Polynesian culture is also known as Havaiki Nui.

As we drove around with Teiva and Matarii, I asked them if anyone on Tahiti was practicing the old religion and traditions or if everyone had been converted to Christianity following the arrival of the missionaries. The next thing we knew, we were hiking up a rough, muddy hill, following a remarkable, very affable local man named

Sunny Walker. He told us that he is descended from the missionary Henry Teuira (who wrote a book about Tahiti in ancient times) and he is the son of the writer Pare Teinaore. He served in the military, was a union activist, and is clearly a humanist with a deep commitment to spirituality, nature, and ancestral ways.

In 1999, Sunny formed a group of friends and relatives and they tried to live in the most traditional way possible. They planted their own food, gathered as much traditional knowledge as they could, organized fishing and canoe building rituals, and culled medicinal plants. This quest for authenticity led them to practice the indigenous religion, which includes animism; it is perhaps the oldest religion in the world. It is a belief that everything — from stones and trees and animals to human works and elements of weather — is alive and has a spirit.

Sunny restored an old *marae* or sacred space, on family land in 2000. He told us that before practicing the ancient religion, he was Protestant, but he felt let down by the religion he was raised in. He starting looking into and studying other religions, and found he was attracted to Taoism and animism, which were similar to ancient Polynesian beliefs and practices. He started to find out more about the latter, and got plenty of opposition from certain members of his family, including a pastor who warned him he was waking up the devil.

But Sunny persisted, and explained that he "did a re-sanctification to wake up the ancestors and the gods." Visitors are invited to come to some of the rituals, "but it is not a tourist activity," Sunny explained. People from around the world have brought him stones, which are incorporated into the *marae*.

"Sunny," I asked, "do you feel the presence of the ancestors, and those who came before you? Are they present at the rituals?"

Sunny nodded, and said he could feel their *mana*.

The following day, I asked Teiva and Matarii if they could talk to us about *mana*. We had heard about it throughout Polynesia, and I understood, in general, that it referred to a kind of supernaturally bestowed spiritual power and prestige; it was often used to speak about an ancestor, or a great chief in the past. But I wanted to meet someone living today who our guides thought had *mana*. And that's when they drove us to meet Patrice Teinauri, a traditional Tahitian healer who they said was very powerful.

He was preparing an *ahi ma'a* (earth oven) to feed his relatives, who were arriving soon. Without asking who we were or why we came, he unwrapped a banana leaf and fed us. Paul asked him if it was all right to take his photo, and he nodded his assent. Patrice looked like a Polynesian healer out of central casting. His eyes shimmered, his face was ringed by a halo of silver hair, and he was dressed in a floral *pareo,* which wrapped around his hips. He had sporadic tattoos on his chest and ankles, and a thick band or belt of tattoos around his waist. He apologized for being busy, and invited us to come back the next day, which of course we did.

We learned that Patrice was one of the men who accompanied Teve to Samoa to get his tattoos, and told us he had been tattooed there as well. But unlike what Teve went through, his were not all done at the same time; he did them bit-by-bit. It was painful, but tolerable. He and Teve were the first people to be tattooed in Samoa, which gives him certain earned prestige there. His belt of tattoos gives him the right to speak and eat at a local king's table if he goes back to Samoa.

He told us that the tattoos were done ceremonially. The tattoo maker stuck an egg in oil and broke it on the forehead of Teve and his two supporters, Patrice, and a third man who I shall call M; the latter also got tattoos. The breaking of the egg established a taboo: the three men were not allowed to shave, have sex, drink alcohol, or curse until the entire ceremony was over.

"The man called M slept with a woman, and the whole village was coming after him," Patrice recalled. "The population would have killed him for not keeping the taboo. Well, for three years after that he suffered, and kept arranging and re-arranging candles; he became almost crazy. He was ready to hang himself. I found him sitting in a dark room, listening to traditional music, and shaking uncontrollably. I thought it was from the taboo. I reminded M about that. I stayed with him for two weeks, and he was healed. We never spoke about it again."

As Patrice spoke, I understood why Matarii and Teiva had brought us to meet him. We were in the presence of someone with strong *mana*.

Patrice told us that he came from the remote Tahitian island of Rurutu, and their god was Aa. "Today Aa is in a museum in London. I and other people from my village in Rurutu still believe in our Aa. Many people still believe in the old gods."

"Patrice, we are actually going to Rurutu on this trip," I said. He smiled and said it was good we were going there.

Paul noticed that Patrice had a *tiki* statue on his land. "Yes," Patrice said. "Our neighbors were having problems. There had been illnesses and deaths. They said they saw the *tiki* walking around, and they complained to the police. The police came to see me. I told the police that I gave them permission to tell my neighbors that they could come and take the *tiki*. They never came."

Patrice asked if we wanted to see where he did his healings. He explained that he does traditional medicine for kidneys and liver, brain tumors, and internal hemorrhoids. He showed us how he uses suction and sharks' teeth from two different kinds of sharks—lemon and teko sharks.

Patrice spoke to us about two skulls that he brought home from a museum in Hawaii. They were supposed to be given to the community, but the mayor of the community refused them. So Patrice took them. He put them in a *tapa* cloth with traditionally made *monoi* oil, and buried them in the hill near his house. It took half an hour to carry them there.

I briefly told Patrice about my history of communicating with the dead. He listened carefully, his eyes wide. Then he said, "Your grandmother comes from the sea. She had a big impact on you."

My grandmother was long gone, but Patrice had no trouble accessing her. He was not at all surprised by the fact that I connected with those who had passed. For him, the world of *tikis*, gods, and other realms were a vital part of his life.

Before we left, Patrice said, "*ti la œ ra te mana*," you are full of power. I felt like crying. I didn't even say thank you. Was he referring to the fact that like him, I lived in a spiritually porous world?

I stayed awake half the night thinking about the things Patrice had told us. I couldn't wait to go to Rurutu, where Aa came from, and I wanted to find out more about traditionally made *monoi* oil, which Patrice had used to bury the skulls.

Monoi (a scented oil) is widely used as a skin moisturizer and softener. Today it is made commercially, and you can buy it in shops and at the airport, but I wanted to try the real deal, and get it from someone who made it from scratch.

We were taken to meet a 77-year-old woman who makes and sells *monoi* oil at her rustic, fairly remote home. Her mother made it, so did her grandmother, and I suspect her grandmother's grandmother made it too. "The secret is to add a few sand crabs or *chevrette* (local shrimp). If you are using shrimp, only include the heads, for fermentation. Besides coconut that is grated and dried in the sun, add *tiare Tahiti* (an aromatic flower)," she said.

After our preparation lesson, she asked if we wanted to visit the tomb of her husband who had died three months before; they had been married for 54 years. We said we would be honored to visit her husband's resting place. She and her son Afai Moana took us there. It was on the same property as her home, a few minutes' walk away. The small hut, covered with palm-like pandanus leaves, was decorated inside with what looked like white marble, but was actually ceramic tile.

We stood for a few minutes in silence. "Is it okay if I ask you a question?" I inquired. She nodded her assent. "Have you gotten a message from your husband since he died?" "Yes," she replied. "I was flying in a plane and I saw him in the window."

"This is the first time she has spoken about that," Afai said. "I am surprised she never told me before. My father was probably protecting my mother. He never liked her to travel far."

"He was right there, in the window. I looked and he was there," she added.

The next day we flew to the remote Tahitian island of Rurutu, in the Astral Island archipelago. Our guide was Yves Gentilhomme; he is a Frenchman who married a local woman, and has devoted several decades of his life to becoming the island's unofficial historian. As we toured the island of 2400 people, Yves showed us how self-sufficient they are. They raise pigs; grow taro as well as noni and other plants for health; make hats from pandanus; gather shells; eat coconuts; and honor their ancestors. "The whole island is an outdoor supermarket," Yves said.

According to Yves, at a Rurutu wedding, where more than one couple often gets married at the same event, everyone comes and relates their genealogy. Historically, genealogy was of the utmost importance and it was central to social position. A person could claim a position of power based on the status of an ancestor. People proudly traced their lineage back to a particular *marae*, a stone platform that held enormous *mana*. It was also the place of the gods, and people prayed there and offered sacrifices.

Yves took us to the tomb of the last king of Rurutu, and commented that "the king was kind of embalmed when he died, so that his *mana* would pass down into the earth and be returned to the earth." Even after his body was gone, the *mana* lived on.

I asked Yves on several occasions about Aa, but he didn't reply. It was clear he didn't want to answer, and I was disappointed. And then, when we were on our way to the airport to leave the island, he turned off the main road and said we were going to visit the only replica left of the most important ancient god Aa; he is sometimes referred to as Tiki Aa. Paul reached for my hand. He was as excited as I was.

The statue, which is in a cabinet in a government office, stands about three and a half feet high, and its ears, mouth, neck, and other parts of its body are made of tiny ancestral figures. "This is the genealogy of the person who had it made. It depicts all the ancestors. There are about 30 on the body. There used to be a compartment on the back of the figure that contained about 24 more. They are all the ancestors. You are looking at a thousand years of Polynesian history right here, in one figure."

Henry Moore was so impressed by Tiki Aa that he cast it in bronze. Picasso also had a copy. "Aa is part of the ancient religion, and it was frowned on by missionaries. They referred to those days as dark times, and people don't talk about it," Yves explained.

Neither Paul nor I said one word about Patrice, and the fact that he said he and many other people still believe in Tiki Aa. My reveries were interrupted by Yves, who said, "ancestors are very important here."

As we drove towards the airport, I reflected that it's sad that, in the United States, most people I have met know little or even nothing about the people that came before them. They may not even know their grandparents' names, or where they came from. In my experience, many immigrants who came to the United States in the early 20th century, or even before, were fleeing persecution, economic hardship, violence, forced conscription, lack of opportunity. They wanted a better, safer life where they would have freedom and the ability to prosper. Many of them wished to put their old lives behind them, and they wanted to raise their children as Americans. They spoke little about where they came from and who came before them. They didn't pass on some of the beliefs, rituals, language, and ways of interacting with people and nature. In succeeding generations, the little information that was known disappeared. The roots from the past were severed. Science, progress, rational thinking, and organized religion replaced a broader, more inclusive, sometimes more indigenous way of interacting with the world, and with other worlds.

In my opinion, much was lost. And I am not unique in thinking that. People everywhere are searching for meaning, for connection, and they often look to ancestral wisdom and ways of living. They consider life a continuum. Existence does not stop with death. And if you are willing, and if the deceased are willing, you can communicate. You can connect to something larger than yourself. You can expand a limited notion of time. You can transcend what was presented to you as a barrier.

In all ways, you are not alone.

Soon you will have a chance to experience it first hand. But first, we have some more traveling to do.

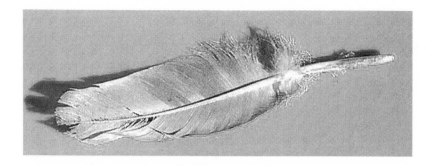

Chapter XVI.

NEW MEXICO, USA, USA

I knew nothing about Bosque Redondo, which is located near Fort Sumner, New Mexico, several hours from where I live. I asked a number of my friends, and they had never heard of it either. And yet, Bosque Redondo is of major importance to the Diné (Navajo) people and the Mescalero Apaches. I think it is of major importance to the rest of us too.

Perhaps you have heard of the Trail of Tears, the forced relocation of Cherokee and other tribal groups in the Southeastern part of the United States to Indian Territory, as it was called (today it is Oklahoma). It is a dark chapter in U.S. history. In 1830 the Indian Removal Act was passed under President Andrew Jackson, and Cherokee and other tribal people were forced to leave their homelands and travel about 2,000 miles to be resettled. Their farms and lands, which were very productive and fertile, could then be occupied and exploited by white settlers.

Thousands of Native Americans died of starvation, exposure, and disease during the very difficult and arduous overland trip. It is a haunting and horrible story of U.S. government policy toward Native people gone very very wrong.

The Bosque Redondo story of cruelty and disregard for Native Americans was directed against the Diné and the Mescalero Apache. The latter were rounded up and brought to the remote Bosque Redondo outpost starting in 1863, and over the next few years, Diné were forced to leave their traditional homeland and march hundreds of miles to the unfamiliar, unwelcoming land. They were never told where they were going. Many perished on what is called the Long Walk. When they arrived at Bosque Redondo, they were made to farm, so they could sustain themselves, but the land was not suitable, the drinking water was brackish and made them sick, and the corn crop failed. Diné began to leave, and in 1868, a treaty was finally made between the U.S. government and the Diné people: they were allowed to begin the Long Walk back to their homeland, and, most important, their sovereignty as the Navajo Nation was recognized.

It is estimated that of the 9,000 people who were forcibly held at Bosque Redondo, 3,000 perished walking there, living there, or on the Long Walk home.

One particularly graphic and awful story was about mothers on the Long Walk who carried starving babies. The mothers gathered herbs and plants, chewed them to make them more digestible, and transferred them from their mouths into their babies' mouths. Like mother birds, I thought. And sometimes the little birds survived and sometimes they perished miserably.

It was 2018, the 150th anniversary of 1868, and Paul and I decided to go to learn about the internment at Bosque Redondo, and to support the people whose ancestors had been so horribly treated before they finally were recognized as a nation.

A guided tour of the Memorial was offered shortly after we arrived, and the park ranger who led it seemed informed and compassionate. Some of the Native American people in our small group were taking detailed notes. The guide said he heard stories of unimaginable corruption. One story was that the head of the internment camp was given $1,000,000 a year to adequately feed the 9,000 internees. And, unforgivably, he pocketed $700,000 while the people starved.

We were told by several Diné people we met on the tour that Diné are not supposed to go to places associated with death and suffering. But some of them, in spite of the taboo, felt it was important to come back to the site of their ancestors' tragedy. An Apache woman also said that her people are not supposed to go to places associated with death. "We are told to look forward, to the future, not backwards. We want to move forward, move on in life. But I feel I must acknowledge what the ancestors lived through."

In the afternoon, Native American dances took place in an outdoor arena, and the announcer said, "the Diné have come today to free the souls of those who suffered here." I sat quietly, watching the dances, trying to absorb what I was learning and pondering what those words could mean.

Soon a man of both Diné and Apache heritage, adorned in beautiful buckskin clothes, walked close to where I was sitting. "May I ask you a question?" I inquired. "Yes, sure," he replied. "Can you tell me what the announcer meant when he said you have come to free the souls?" "We are all traumatized, all of us," he explained. "We carry the trauma inside of us, and we have to free ourselves of it so the ancestors can rest and they can have peace and we can have peace."

I thought about his words and asked, "So how can you free yourselves?" "By coming here, back to the site. By allowing ourselves to be here, by dancing, by acknowledging our ancestors and what they endured."

"Do you think the ancestors are here today?" "Yes. For sure."

When it was time for dinner, Paul walked up to a woman who was selling homemade tamales. I waited for him to return, but it took him almost half an hour. When he finally came back he said the woman told him about the trauma of her family, and how it had affected her and impacted her life.

We began to talk to an Apache woman who explained that she was dancing for the ancestors. "Are they present here today?" I asked. "Of course they are," she replied. "When I dance, they can feel it."

That night, when it got dark, a small troupe of Apache crown dancers built a fire, and then began to dance in full regalia. I had seen similar dancers 25 years before, and I never forgot the power of them dancing around the bonfire. The announcer asked all the people present to come in close to the dancers, and, if they wished, to touch the dancers for healing. Everyone inched closer. "The spirits can heal you," the announcer said. The spectators, almost all of whom were Native Americans, reached out to touch the performers. "The dancers are men, but they are also spirits," the man next to me said, his eyes fixed on them. It was an entrancing act of transformation from the human realm to the spiritual realm that sometimes takes place during indigenous ceremonies, and even presentational dances. It may draw in the spectators as well, so they go from being observers to becoming participants, even though they are not dancing. It's as though the ceremonial dancers know how to call in, connect to, and propitiate the spirits of the earth. It is a great contribution to our shared humanity.

A week later, Paul and I went to a Navajo rug auction in Crownpoint, New Mexico. Not only is it a place to buy dazzling Navajo rugs, but it's also an opportunity to meet the weavers. Some of them are older women who speak no English, and they patiently sit there, adorned in magnificent pleated skirts and turquoise and silver jewelry, waiting for the auction to begin. Two of them that we met do all the work themselves: they raise the sheep, shear them, card and spin the wool to make their weavings. Each of the works they produce is almost alive with the time, energy, and care they have put into it.

I spoke to the daughter of one of them, who graciously offered to translate. I mentioned to her that we had been to Bosque Redondo. Her eyes grew wide with interest, and when I told her that Paul had some photos on his cell phone, she said she would love to see them. She reiterated what we had heard at the event; Diné were not supposed to go there, but she was very curious about it and considered going herself. She said her mother didn't want to go.

Paul showed the daughter photos of the Apache dancers at night, and the woman excitedly shared the images with her mother. The women looked at the photos very slowly and carefully, taking in all the details of the dancers, the bonfire, and the inky night sky. "I don't think my mother will change her mind," she said in a whisper. "When our ancestors left Bosque Redondo, the man who signed the treaty said no Diné should ever go back there. There was so much pain. But still, one day I think I want to go."

Our conversation ended after that because the auction started. When we left, we waved goodbye to the women. I wondered if the daughter would go back to Bosque Redondo, and if she would feel the presence of her traumatized ancestors. I am pretty sure the answer is yes.

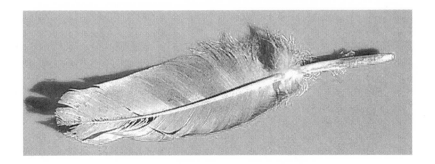

Chapter XVII.

NEW ZEALAND, BULGARIA, NORWAY

A Chinese friend of mine looked at me quizzically when I asked her if she is open to communicating with the dead. She doesn't like to talk about death, so I quickly dropped the subject. But when I looked at her, I saw that she was crying. I have known her for twenty years, and I have never seen her cry before.

I gently asked what was wrong, and she said she missed her mother, who had passed away decades before. "She was such a kind woman. She took care of people. She was good to everyone."

I put my arm around her, and she continued crying and talking. She said that when her mother died, she had buried her with paper objects that she could later use. The objects were burned at the time of her funeral.

I recalled that, when Paul and I were in Taiwan, we entered a shop that sold paper computers, houses, furniture, coats, toys, shirts, TVs, food, and many other utilitarian objects. When we inquired, the owner said that these would be burned at funerals, so that the dead could use them in the future, in the next life.

In Egypt, we had seen ancient *ushabti* figurines among the antiquities in the archeology museum in Cairo. In ancient Egypt, they were placed in tombs alongside of other grave goods that were offerings for the deceased. The *ushabti* were servants that the dead could use in the afterlife in case they had to perform manual labor or do anything physically strenuous.

In Northland, New Zealand, between the entrances of the Whangape Harbour to the north and Hokianga, is a small village called Mitimiti. It is such a memorable and lyrical name that we asked a local guide what it meant. He said it could be translated as "lick lick." He showed us a flat rock where, according to tradition, a fierce battle took place. The powerful tribal leader or chief, named More Te Korohanga, was slain. Those were cannibal days, and his body was put on the rock and dismembered. The warriors of the victorious tribe wanted to consume part of his body to get his *mana*. Soon there were no dismembered parts left, so those who didn't get their share licked his blood from the rock, and thereby got the chief's *mana*. The name Mitimiti preserves the memory of this event.

A local woman told us another version. The name referred to a belief among the Maori that the thirsty souls of the dead paused at Mitimiti to lick or lap up the water of a stream on their way to Cape Reinga, where they entered the underworld.

In Bulgaria recently, we stayed in a guesthouse in the village of Gorno Draglishte and dined on homemade treats prepared by two delightful *babas*, or grandmas, named Jana and Elena. It was very sweet and not at all hokey when they dressed us in traditional clothes, and sang Bulgarian songs for us, making sure to incorporate the name of our home city into one song. It was Maundy Thursday, and they colored Easter eggs with us. They said the first egg they made was colored red, to symbolize the blood of Jesus.

While we drank *rakia,* an alcoholic beverage made from grapes, and savored the grated potato pie, sausages, sour cabbage, vegetable mish mash and *banitsa* (a tasty pastry made of cheese and eggs stuffed inside filo dough), we talked about the past, present, future, the history of Bulgaria, and what people do for Easter. "In church, people crawl under the table," one of the *babas* said.

"Crawl under the table?" I asked. "What is that about?" Our guide and translator said it was a big nothing. "You know," he said, "a table, and people crawl under it. That's it. No big deal."

Of course we insisted that the next day, which was Good Friday, we go to a local Bulgarian Orthodox church. When we entered, all the chandeliers were lit, and candles burned brightly. A service was taking place, and the participants stood for the duration.

Near the front of the church, a table, covered with a red cloth that bore the image of Jesus, was set up. People lined up to crawl under the table for health and wellbeing. I got in line. "May I ask what the table is for?" I asked the couple behind me. "It is Jesus's tomb, his coffin," the woman replied. "We go inside to mourn Jesus and connect to him. We feel his presence very strongly."

To the left of the table, a few older women, who said they couldn't stand for the entire service, sat in wooden choir stall seats. They held flowers and leaves in their hands, and they saw me staring at their hands, wondering what the flowers were for. Without any words, one of them gave me a green leaf. Others saw her doing this, and they all gave me flowers. My eyes filled with tears from the simple, spontaneous act of generosity. The women pointed to a long line of people waiting to place the flowers on the altar. I got in line and everyone parted to make way so I, the stranger, could advance to the front of the line. A man told me the flowers were an offering to Jesus. He said that for them, Jesus was an eternally alive, living presence.

For the ancient Vikings, belief in the afterlife was a given. At the Viking Ship Museum in Oslo, Norway, we saw the magnificent Osberg ship, which took 21 years to restore. The vessel was probably built in 820 C.E., and was used for the ship burial of two high status women about 14 years later. One of the women was probably in her 70's or 80's, suffered from arthritis, and likely died painfully of cancer. The other was younger, maybe about 50, and the cause of her death is unknown. It has even been suggested that the younger woman was a sacrificed slave of the older woman, and that the latter may have been the grandmother of the first king of Norway.

The two women were laid on a bed that was made up with bed linens, and they were given a staggering number of burial gifts to accompany them to the afterlife. The objects included four elaborately designed sleighs and a carved wooden cart; kitchen utensils, a frying pan, beds, tents, and spinning tools; fifteen horses, six dogs, two small cows; apples, blueberries and bread dough; horse shoes and dog chains; chests, barrels and a quartz stone.

In Viking lore, Valhalla is the afterlife realm for heroes who died in battle. The women known as the Valkyries gather warriors from the battlefields where they fell, and bring them to Valhalla, Odin's great hall, where they pour mead for them.

A few years ago, after visiting the Viking Ship Museum, through a miraculous concatenation of events, I found myself in Gudvangen, Norway. There, in the bosom of a fjord, under a sky of cotton ball clouds, 500 authentically Viking-clad re-enactors from 20 nations brought the Vikings back to life. Bearded Georg Olafr Reydarsson

Hansen, in a fur-trimmed hat, with a large sword in a scabbard at his waist, sailed up in a Viking ship to oversee the event. As I walked around, I met needle binders, blacksmiths, a fire juggler, rune crafters, a poet who uses Old Norse metric forms, sword fighters, actors, cooks, potters, candle makers, artists, furniture artisans, and leatherworkers who congregated to learn, exchange information, eat, sleep, perfect their crafts and have fun. In real life, whatever that means, they are scholars, miners, jewelers, traders, administrators, students, businesspeople, teachers, marine archeologists, cartoonists, and musicians.

These modern-day Vikings were so close to the real thing that I wondered if they weren't reincarnations of the old Vikings. When I finally asked four or five of them if they thought they had been Vikings in a past lifetime, they didn't laugh or snicker at the question: in fact, they readily said yes.

Many of them have Viking names, eat Viking foods, and travel to every Viking market and craft show they can find to interact with others like them. They have mates who are Viking enthusiasts, study Viking legends and lore, and a few of them have landed jobs as guides to authenticated Viking archeological sites.

About three hours into our visit, a man named Lars Magnar Enoksen tapped me on the shoulder. Not only does he write books on Vikings and runes and coach young athletes in the ancient sport of Glima wrestling, but he is also a Viking magician. "Are you interested in learning about Viking magic?" he asked me. "Yes," I replied, "Of course. Yes." "Good. Then I would like to invite you to a late-night sorcery class, which will happen when all the visitors have left. This is the final class where students who have studied with me for three years are going to learn and use a Galdur, or Viking oral incantation."

Later that evening, inside a small wooden cabin, a dozen of us sat around a blazing fire, conjuring. The other eleven wore Viking attire, and were familiar with Norse metrics, poems and ancient language – a deep rumbling as if from the core of the earth. It wasn't necessary to understand everything that was being said at our Viking coven. I could feel the meaning and the intensity of the participants.

With a mischievous glint in his eye, Lars revealed that Galdurs can invoke evil (*onde*), and sorcerers can, with relish, use them against their enemies. But that night, Lars's male and female witches were very clear that they wanted to craft an incantation that would be for the common good (*gode*).

After hours of honing their intentions, the student sorcerers fashioned a seven-line Galdur that asked for wisdom, human warmth, and friendship to dissolve any tension in the Viking camp. Lars gently guided them to make it shorter, simpler, more abbreviated, more alliterative, forceful, and poetic. After more hours, the sorcerer's apprentices decided that they wanted to focus on wind, fire, and the mother of the earth. They agreed on the following incantation:

Vinde varme (warm wind)

Mektige moder (mighty mother)

Bringe viden for alle (bring wisdom for all)

Bringe venskap for alle (bring friendship for all)

We repeated the magic spell silently, until we had memorized it and then, like ducklings, followed Lars out into the crisp night air. He walked us to the edge of the fjord, and made us circle around a large granite stone. No one spoke. We looked up at the sliver of moonlight in the sky and passed around a horn full of mead. We drank from it and then spat it out on a rock; the mead and our spittle were offerings of drink and bodily fluids to the earth. Then, under Lars's tutelage, we began the incantation: tentatively at first, and then, with each repetition, building in confidence and volume. The rock faces of the fjord echoed as we roared our incantation up to the heavens. There was a flash of lightning. The man next to me said it meant we were heard.

Galdurs are oral incantations, and written versions were inscribed on runes. Lars told me something that made me realize the power of the sorcerer's words. If a word ended in a letter and the next word began with the same letter (i.e. Lars Skriver), it was forbidden to write the two words separately; they had to be written together (i.e. Larskriver), thus eliminating one of the repeated letters. Unless, of course, you wanted to incant. In that case, the sound of a letter uttered twice has a hypnotic, trance-inducing, magical effect.

Galdurs were considered so powerful that, in the 1330's, the Norwegian archbishop of Trondheim banned them. If you were caught incanting, you were expelled from society, and anyone was allowed to kill you. In Iceland in the 1600's, they didn't burn many female witches; instead, they burned Galdur-men.

Lars explained that, when making a Galdur, you might call out to male or female gods, or both. You are asking for power and, in order to receive it, you have to give something up — like physical or mental power. "I run until I am exhausted before making Galdurs," Lars said. "I give my power away and ask to receive it back in another form. It is a circuit. It fertilizes you. You give something away to the gods of nature, and when it comes back to you, it is strengthened by them. Then you give it away again and receive it back in a continuous process. This makes both you and the gods gain from it."

I found myself haunted by the old Norse incantations. Thanks to Lars, a modern-day sorcerer, I was able to taste the nectar of magic that is hidden and enfolded in the ancient verses and writings of the Vikings. There is a lot more to the Viking culture than raiding and marauding. There is farming, a proto democracy, and important roles for women. There is also deep magic, and elaborate preparation for the afterlife. And if you die heroically in battle, there is Valhalla.

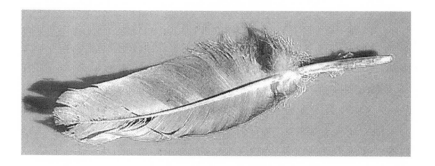

Chapter XVIII.

VANUATU

It is entirely possible that you have never heard of Vanuatu. It is made up of 83 islands, where 113 languages are spoken, and when I visited, approximately 270,000 people lived there. Vanuatu is roughly located between Fiji and Papua New Guinea. Christianity is the norm, but below the surface is a deep belief in animism, a world where stones speak and everything in nature is alive. Cannibalism was still practiced in Vanuatu until about 40 years ago, and some say more recently than that. But be assured that we found Vanuatu as hospitable and safe as it is exotic.

Customs may vary from village to village and island to island, and I will only tell you things that I personally saw or were told to me directly.

On the remote island of Malekula, which is only visited by .01 per cent of the people who come to Vanuatu, we were plunged into an unfamiliar and fascinating world. We learned that if a husband really loves his wife, he knocks out her front teeth. Actually, someone else does it for him, using a stone. So every time we saw a big toothless smile, we assumed that the woman was really loved.

But don't think the women are devalued. In fact, we were told that peace came to enemy tribes that practiced cannibalism because of the women. As one woman explained it, "The two warring chiefs were not going to stop the violence. They were too macho. But if a woman was married to a man from the enemy tribe, or if she had another strong connection, she could go to see the enemy chief. She would ask if he was willing to make peace. If he was, then they picked a date, and when the chiefs met, kava was drunk to mellow everyone out and there was an exchange of gifts. It was because of women and their intervention that the violence could cease."

When we were asked if we wanted to visit a cannibal site, we braced ourselves for the grisly, and went. We saw rocks that were used for cooking a warrior who was eaten there. His right arm was given to the chief, who had to eat it separately, not around other people. The chief had an in-ground oven, and a big stone where he sat and ate. We saw some degraded bones, which were leftovers.

There was cannibal etiquette, and it was somewhat of a relief to find out that women weren't eaten. Also, cannibals generally consumed just the arms and legs and threw away the rest. The meat eaters had to wear sticks in their hair to scratch lice; after eating human flesh, they couldn't scratch with their hands, or the spirits would kill them. Also, after eating a human, a man couldn't touch a child or sleep with his wife for 30 days. He slept for 30 days at the *nakamal*, the traditional meeting place, which was generally only for males. They washed their hands with water mixed with special leaves to chase away the spirits. Then they were purified.

We were then taken to a sanctuary site where chiefs were buried. The chief was first buried sitting up, with his head above ground. After

30 days, his skull was moved to the sanctuary site and placed under a tilted stone. Every tomb at the sanctuary site has a skull and a conch shell; the latter was used in life to communicate and call people together. The sanctuary site is a place where a chief prays when he is alive. And only chiefs can visit the site. Our guide, Etienne, said, "I think the soul of the tribe remains here."

On Port Vila, which is the main island and one most visitors fly into, we visited Iarofa village. Chief Johnson is committing his life to teaching young people about their heritage. Raised by his grandparents, he was blessed with deep tribal knowledge.

Johnson pointed to a thatched wooden house and asked me how long I thought it took to build it in ancient days. "Several days? A week? I have no idea," I replied. Then he held up a stone axe, and asked me how long I thought it took to make that. I shrugged helplessly as he demonstrated how difficult it was to try to shape something only using a stone. "We do not know how long it took," he said, "because the song is lost. They sang a song that gave them strength and endurance, and it called in spirits to intervene and help them. We will never know how long it took to make the stone axe. The house took seven to eight years."

For the next few hours, Johnson showed us the brilliance of Stone Age technology. We saw branches that were used to extract a cotton-like fiber, and others that naturally stored water. Leaves were twisted to make a fishing line, and a chicken bone was attached for a hook. The golden spider was very useful; its web was used for fishing line because it was very gluey and fish got stuck to it. Resin was put into a dead fish's eye; if it turned white, it meant the fish was toxic. Another plant was put into the intestines of a toxic fish to make it non-toxic.

We walked to another place in the woods of the village where they performed fire dances. First we saw a series of dances where the dancers carried clubs and sang spiritual songs whose words they didn't understand. A warrior would leave the village for nine months and receive the songs in dreams. One dancer got the words from his deceased grandmother in a dream.

We were fortunate to be invited to a circumcision ceremony, which also includes a bride-price ceremony. The groom's family piled up gifts that would be offered to pay for a bride. Bananas. Root crops. Mats. *Pareos* (wraparound skirts). Pandanus baskets. Kava roots. Pigs. The pile was enormous, and everyone in the village witnessed that the bride price had been paid. Then gifts for the uncle of the circumcision boy were piled up. He was present for the boy's birth and for his first hair cutting. He has enormous responsibility for the boy, including his first shaving and future marriage, and he has been paid with gifts along the way. The boy's mother has been saving since the boy's birth to be able to gift the uncle on the day of the circumcision ceremony.

That night, we came back for the evening events. I spent a long time talking to Jimmy, a very articulate man who was sitting next to me on a mat. "Perhaps you think we are ignorant and undeveloped and superstitious, but we have a lot in our favor. Take our tribal economics and social organization, for example. We may be poor, but no one is living on the street. Everyone has a house; in fact, I have three. We have all the food we need. So what does the word 'poor' mean? If there is a problem or conflict, the chief resolves it. If you commit a crime, you pay for it with pigs, kava, yams, and so forth."

Jimmy sighed and said that money is changing their lives. "Now people want money for clothes and tools and trucks. We have to depend on what we know, and what our ancestors taught us. Here, inland, *kastom* (traditional culture) is preserved. People shouldn't give up what they have. Traditional ways and knowledge and wisdom are much more important than money and possessions."

A chief on Tanna Island also explained to us about economics. "You make the last life ceremony before you die — this is only for men. You pay for the burial in advance. If you die before you can make a ceremony, your family makes it. When a man dies, it is the last payment to his family. His family paid for his bride price. When he dies, his family is paid back."

On Tanna Island, we were also introduced to two so-called cargo cults. The popular perception is that adherents built replicas of American airfields, and performed elaborate rituals to bring cargo to them — the goodies they first saw when U.S. troops landed there in World War II. But the very name "cargo cult" diminishes what they really are. And on a Friday night, Chief Isaak, the paramount chief of the John Frumm cult, taught us a very different version.

In his village, which had about 300 inhabitants, Chief Isaak, who was 72 years old, accompanied us to a hut where we sat on mats, waiting, as it grew dark outside. When there was no light at all, we heard lilting string music coming toward us. Then we heard a distinct tapping on wood and out of the dark people emerged, entered the hut, and sat on mats on the floor. They began playing guitars and singing, and were accompanied by someone who played a drum that was made from a truck part. It sounded like church music, but none of the songs was recognizable. Chief Isaak said the gathering and singing takes place every Friday and lasts all night.

He spoke softly, and explained to us about John Frumm (it rhymes with "broom"). He first appeared to Isaak's father in 1930. He was a white man with white hair. He came again during World War II, when the United States had a large military presence in Vanuatu. The local people saw trucks, vehicles, food, furniture, and radios arriving on Tanna Island from the U.S. "John Frumm promised that he would come back and send cargo. He knew what we needed. I don't want the cargo as much as I want John to come back," the chief said. Every day he waits with messianic fervor and devotion for the return of John Frumm. Every day they raise the U.S. marine and navy flags, and the flag of the U.S. government. On February 15th there are military parades; they imitate the U.S military with improvised drums, trumpets and uniforms.

As Chief Isaak spoke, it became clear that there are many levels to the John Frumm cult: spiritual, material, cultural, messianic, and mystical. Isaak said that John Frumm speaks to him and gives him messages, for example, about peace, helping others, and not stealing. "He also speaks to the people who write the songs you are hearing tonight; that is how they write their songs. John is on the road. He will come and then Jesus will come."

Isaak says that the Americans helped to free the people from colonial laws against *kastom* practices, and now they can maintain their culture and traditions, so they raise the American flag in thanks.

I asked if it mattered that John Frumm might not be alive any more. "He will come. He promised to bring cargo and said he would return. After he left, the people got iceboxes, pigs, and kava, and business improved. They got what they asked for. What he promised was true. He will return, even though it hasn't happened yet."

On Espiritu Santo Island (popularly called Santo), we went to our second burial site for chiefs; the first had been on Malekula. On Santo we learned from a local guide that when the chief dies, they place his body on a stone slab. The people live there for 100 days and eat there. They consume anything that comes out of the body of the chief, like worms. The body of the chief has strong spirit, knowledge, and skill. When they eat these things, they get the chief's attributes inside of them. They believe that after a chief dies, he will live in a different world, where he will be the chief of those who died. And his son becomes chief of the living.

Towards the end of our stay on Vanuatu, we met with paramount Chief Tom, who spoke very openly about the soul of his culture on Tanna Island. He explained that chiefs are not politicians; they are born chiefs, not elected. They are like judges and kings, and their job is to protect custom, culture, land, and language.

He said, "All life came from the spirit world, and an evolution took place. Some spirits became stones. Some changed into human beings. The stones travelled all over Tanna, outside of Tanna, to other countries, and then came back. Only a few of the people today know the names of the stones they come from. This knowledge has been passed down from generation to generation but is being forgotten. Only a few still know the names of the stones that became humans. Some stones became huge stones, and others became birds."

I shivered as he told us three of the names that came from the spirit world. "The world is on the wrong track, and it is time to reveal many secrets," he explained.

The last person we met was a *kleva,* which means a healer or sorcerer, from Malekula. His name was Alben, and he told us some deep and mysterious things about Vanuatu. "When you die," he said in a low voice, "if your eyeball is gone after three days, it means your spirit is going to a new life. If your eyeball is still there, you're not going anywhere."

Alben told us about his specialty as a *kleva*. He makes a date with the nature that surrounds his home, and on that date he goes to a secret place where he talks to nature to get power. He connects back to the creation of the world by God; it was good, and God blessed it, so all of nature is a blessing.

Alben can talk to stones. They have a special stone to calm the seas and stop rain, and another to bring rain. He gets a special leaf, rubs it on a stone, and says certain words to the stone. Stones have power. There is also a special stone to help women in the hospital when they are in labor. Only his family knows the words to say to stones. There are many *klevas* in his village now because he has taught his sisters, brothers, and children. "It's in our blood," he explained.

After we left Vanuatu, I thought about what I had learned. It is a world of permeability, with many levels that operate together or simultaneously. Humans are not just bound by being born and dying. There is life beyond death, and in life there is communication with the spirit world, animals, stones, and the deceased.

They are economically poor, to be sure, but, as Jimmy said, "What does poor mean?"

Chapter XIX.

CZECH REPUBLIC AND GERMANY

I always say, jokingly, that, "I live to leave." I'm addicted to travel. For as long as I remember, I have been fascinated by other cultures. Not only do I learn bits and pieces from people in Japan, Vanuatu, Israel, Brazil, Tahiti, Egypt, Mexico, New Mexico, New Zealand, Italy, and every other place I go, but I also get to fit the pieces together, like a non-material jigsaw puzzle. What emerges is a picture, which is still far from complete, about how other cultures, over time, view the universe and our role in it. I am, quite literally, always learning about life and death.

Several decades ago, the Jewish quarter in Prague grabbed my soul and shook it. The lugubrious cemetery was filled with headstones leaning towards each other and tilted at odd angles as they sank slowly into the yielding earth. No one could tell me how many layers of stones there were, or how many generations of dead slept beneath the visible stones that protruded from the earth.

I stood for a long time at the tomb of 16th century Rabbi Judah Loew, who is known as the Maharal of Prague and who is believed to have created the golem. The golem was made from clay or mud, and it was intended to help the Jews, but it turned into a sort of destructive Frankenstein monster that had to be deactivated.

Many stories and versions of stories are told about the golem. When it was good and well behaved, it could become invisible in order to help people. Every week, Rabbi Loew would de-activate the golem for Sabbath so it could rest. It is said that the golem still lives in the attic of the Old New Synagogue in Prague, although it's closed to the public. The story goes that anyone who looks on it will die.

Few people were in the cemetery, and Rabbi Loew's tomb was dotted with paper *kvittleh;* the petitioners begged him to intervene in matters of love, healing, and success.

I never forgot the power of that cemetery visit, and the story of a rabbi who could not only communicate from beyond the tomb, but could actually create life.

Recently I went back to the Jewish quarter again with Paul; I wanted to show him the cemetery I had told him so much about. During my first visit, it was in Czechoslovakia, but today it's in the Czech Republic. When we arrived, I felt an unexpected shock. Hoards of tourists clogged the streets of the Jewish quarter, which is now one of Prague's top tourist attractions. They came from China and Israel, South America and New Zealand. Some rolled through the streets on Segways and skateboards, and others snapped selfies in the synagogues and cemetery. A catering truck was decorated with a painting of the golem in an apron, and tourists giddily bought golem T-shirts, hats, and plastic figurines.

In spite of this, Paul grew very silent, absorbing the mystical environment created by the stones in the cemetery, and pausing in front of the Maharal's tomb, as I had done so many years before. I don't know what he was thinking at the time, but Paul is fascinated by the weird, and I suspect he was imagining a rabbi who brought earth to life.

Also in Prague, many visitors make pilgrimages to the tomb of Franz Kafka (1883-1924), the famous writer whose fantastical, surreal novels and stories established him as a literary master of the complex, anxiety-ridden inner life we humans generally keep hidden. Like the pious, religious Rabbi Loew, Kafka, who was a secular Jew, can still fulfill wishes from the beyond. Parents sometimes ask Kafka to make their children as brilliant as he was. And I can imagine that more than a few writers have gone there to get inspiration.

After Prague, I wanted to show Kazimierz (the Jewish section of Krakow since the Middle Ages) to Paul. I was surprised at how much it had changed since my first visit, years before, when it was sleepy, sad, and evocative. Now it's a trendy, sort of bohemian part of the city, with Jewish-themed bars, restaurants, tourist shops, and gaggles of tourists everywhere.

I remembered seeing several ancient houses of worship in the area on my first visit, especially the Remuh synagogue— a small, intact 16th century synagogue that is still active. I recalled the adjacent, restored 16th to 17th century cemetery whose headstones had been badly damaged by the Nazis during World War II; the fragments of tombstones that could not be restored had been assembled to create a "wailing wall."

On our recent visit, I heard a new story about Rabbi Moses Isserles, who was known by a Hebrew acronym, which was pronounced "Remuh." We were standing in front of the famous rabbi's tomb and a local guide told us that, according to legend, if you demolished the grave of the Remuh you would die at once. So the Nazis, who were superstitious, left it alone. Today people petition the deceased holy man for help by leaving hand-written prayers at his tomb.

On another occasion, we were in Bayreuth, Germany, to attend Richard Wagner's Ring Cycle. It's a marathon 16 hours of opera spread over four nights, and it's possibly the hardest cultural ticket in the world to get. The average wait is 10 years and then, if you are lucky, you get to sit on the Festspeilhaus's original 19th century wooden seats, in the theatre Wagner himself built, and marvel at music that often seems more divine than human in origin.

What's shocking and baffling is that Wagner composed such music; by most accounts, he was a pretty awful human being. He milked his friends like cash cows, carried on with their wives, lived high on the hog, was foppish in dress, and had his benefactors pay for his pink and green silks and magnificent lodgings. He was also a rabid anti-Semite, and the only one in his entourage more anti-Semitic was his second wife, Cosima, the daughter of Franz Liszt.

Until recently, Wagner fans and Wagner Society members made light of his anti-Semitism. From my personal experience, they deflected questions, or lightheartedly cited a few Jews he worked with, and as if there were a big Wagner rug, the issue was swept under it.

But the day we arrived, we learned how radically things have changed. We climbed the verdant hill to the famous Festspielhaus where the festival performances were first held under the watchful eye and direction of Wagner himself.

Below the theatre, in a large, two-tiered garden, is a very explicit exhibit about Wagner's anti-Semitism. It features prominent metal panels with pictures of Jews who were not allowed to sing, play music, or direct in the Wagner theater in Bayreuth, and tragic stories about what eventually happened to them. Some escaped, some died in concentration camps, and all of them were barred from practicing their craft. In some instances they weren't even Jewish but were married to Jews, or they were one fourth Jewish, but it didn't make a difference. Wagner considered Jews to be evil and anti-cultural and the Germans were the bringers of light and culture.

Even more damning than the Wagner panels are the ones about Cosima. She established stringent rules after Wagner died, not allowing anyone of any Jewish persuasion to have anything to do with the opera except if he or she were a big star. Some members of Wagner's family became friendly with Hitler and the Nazis and turned the festival into a Nazi showcase, which Hitler, an ardent Wagner fan, attended. It's even suggested that the Wagner family's writings and anti-Semitism helped to influence Hitler to discover the final solution to eliminate the Jews.

A Jewish woman we met at the exhibit stood in front of one of the panels, and tears cascaded slowly down her cheek. She placed a flower at the foot of the panel. It seemed clear that somehow she was mourning the death of the person depicted on the panel. Then she walked over to a bust of Wagner and spoke to him in a low voice. Her lips were curled into a sneer, and she cursed him for what he had done. "I hope he can hear me," she said. "I know that wherever he is, he must be suffering for what he did here on earth."

The exhibit was supposed to be temporary, but there has been such support that it is now permanent, so you can see it any time you visit Bayreuth.

But the exhibit was not the only unexpected find in Bayreuth; the other occurred when we met Felix Gothart, the likeable, knowledgeable leader of the Bayreuth Jewish community. He's a tall, fit, gray-haired man, who was sporting a *kippah* (skullcap), jeans, a black jacket with a brown V-neck sweater underneath, and black shades. The original Jewish community members had been sent to concentration and death camps, and suffered the horrific fate imposed by the Nazis. But a new community was born, and Gothart said it has about 500 members, most of which arrived from Russia after the fall of Communism in 1991. Gothart had just finished a remodel of the synagogue.

He drove us to the Jewish cemetery, about 10 minutes away. It was like entering an enchanted forest of the dead, carpeted in green plants and silent except for the occasional chirping of birds. Three stones stand as witnesses to those who died in both world wars, with the addition of an evocative, mystical quote from Ezekiel: "I blow my spirit into you, and you will be alive."

The cemetery, which dates back to 1786, is closed to the public, and Gothart said he only takes people there once a year, on November 9th, to commemorate *Kristallnacht* (it means "the night of broken glass," and refers to a wave of anti-Jewish violence in November, 1938, when many Jews were murdered or incarcerated, and their property was ransacked and destroyed). "The Nazis started removing headstones here, and then stopped. No one knows why. There are about 1,000 stones."

As we walked slowly through the cemetery, Gothart very simply, and movingly, explained that, "All the clearing and cleaning in the cemetery is done by hand. There are no machines inside the walls. Once a year, a machine comes outside the wall and takes what we have cleaned up in the cemetery. They reduce it to mulch, which is then returned to the cemetery. So nothing is removed. This place belongs to the dead. I don't want people to come here to disturb them." He spoke as though the dead were living; I sensed that to him their spirits are still alive. When I asked him, he nodded.

The wall of the cemetery is made of commemorative stones for those who died in Nazi camps. "There are no headstones for them," Gothart said, "because there are no bodies. The dead here have no descendants."

In the old part of the cemetery, all the tombstones are similar, with no difference between rich and poor. Over time, the stones of the wealthy became more elaborate but now they are going back to the old way, where all are equal in death.

We walked past one headstone that Felix pointed out; it belongs to Josef Rubinstein. He was a great admirer of Wagner, and wrote to the great composer to explain that he came from a wealthy Jewish family, was a pianist, transcribed musical scores, and wanted to work for the master. Not one to turn down the lure of someone independently wealthy who could work for him for free, Wagner agreed. Rubinstein became Wagner's personal pianist and transcriber and, by some accounts, was treated poorly. Yet, when Rubenstein heard that Wagner had died, he killed himself. And, inexplicably, Cosima had his body brought to the Jewish cemetery.

Before leaving the cemetery, we had to wash our hands in rainwater, which was kept in a plastic barrel. As Gothart poured the water over my hands with a plastic watering can, I inquired of him, "Why are you doing all of this for the Jewish community?"

"It's like when you light a candle. The flame always goes up. By doing good things you hope, bit by bit, to go up, up, nearer to *Hashem* (God). Humans are not perfect, but what *Hashem* gave us is."

I thought about the Jewish belief that parts of the soul leave the body during sleep, and, if all is well, return to the body when the person wakes up. It's almost like a mini death at night, and rebirth in the morning, for which we are grateful. Hands are washed upon leaving a cemetery to separate the living from the dead. But maybe the separation is an illusion, for the souls of the dead are always accessible…if you know how to reach them.

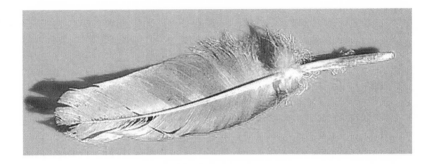

Chapter XX.

JEWS AND THE AFTERLIFE

It may surprise many people to learn that not only does Jewish practice include contacting the dead, but, in the words of Rabbi Jacub Ropp, from San Diego, "We Jews not only believe in an afterlife, but see it as our primary existence. As it says in the Ethic of the Fathers, 'this physical existence is nothing but a preparation for our true spiritual existence that occurs after we leave our physical bodies...The Talmud explains that this world is the world of preparation, the next world is Shabbat [Sabbath] where we eat the fruits of our labor but cannot create anew.'"

It may come as an even greater surprise that there is also a Jewish belief in reincarnation.

A returned soul is called a *gilgul*. You don't get to pick and choose whether you want to return as a *gilgul*. You are not the decider but, rather, it is part of the life-death-reincarnation cycle.

A *gilgul* comes back to get it right, to correct mistakes and actions. If you steal, you come back to return what you stole. You may also come back to complete what wasn't done, to fix things, to work on your character and correct the times you failed to act.

There are also wise, high beings that come back at specific times and for specific purposes to help out. They don't have to go through the death and rebirth cycle. For them, it's just in and out.

In days gone by, some of the rabbis in Europe performed past-life readings.

Further back in time, according to the Hebrew Bible, the prophets Elijah and Elisha could bring people back from the dead.

It is said that every Sabbath, the famous Rabbi Yehuda Ha Nasi came back from the dead to say *kiddish*, the blessing over the wine.

It is sometimes postulated that Moses was reincarnated Abel, who was killed by his brother Cain. Cain was a farmer and Abel was a shepherd, and they both made sacrifices to God. Cain brought the fruit of the soil, and Abel sacrificed the firstborn of his flock. God favored Abel's offering, and Cain killed him out of envy, competition, and sibling rivalry. Like Cain, who was condemned to wander the earth, Moses wandered with his people in the desert for 40 years. And Rebekah, the wife of patriarch Isaac, was Sarah reincarnated. She was the original foremother and the wife of Abraham.

When I was growing up my grandmother, who hailed from a tiny village in Eastern Europe, would always talk about the *Olam Ha Ba Ah* — the world to come, where things would be better. Whenever there was a seemingly insoluble problem, she had confidence it would be solved in the *Olam Ha Ba Ah*. The world seemed to be in a state of chaos? It would get straightened out in the *Olam Ha Ba Ah*.

She had full confidence she would see my father in the *Olam Ha Ba Ah*, and she said that I would too. I'm not rushing to get there, but when my time comes, I hope my traveling and learning will continue before I come back again in any shape or form or even formlessly to get whatever I did wrong right.

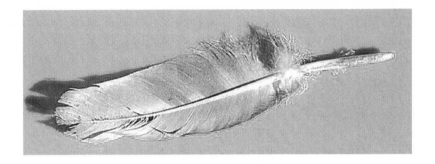

Chapter XXI.

FRANCE AND SANTA FE

As I mentioned at the beginning of the book, communicating with the dead has actually been a secret part of my life for many years ever since that day when I was 20 years old and my father spoke to me in the cemetery. I have shared with you experiences I had around the world with healers who channeled the dead; animists whose teachers were the trees; spirits of the dead who chase the living on mountaintops; the way the dead can come back through electricity; people whose prayers were answered by wise men who are long deceased. I have told you how I requested a sign from my mother before she died. At the time, she sniffed with scorn, but then her spirit returned unmistakably in the form of many white feathers. They appeared on my friend's car, on another friend's windowsill, and once four friends of mine were having dinner in a restaurant in Mexico when a white feather floated down and landed on their table. But what I didn't tell you about were two times when feathers were the conduit for deceased people I didn't personally know.

The first incident happened in Santa Fe when my inspired and soulful teacher, Satpurka, asked me to stay after the end of a *kundalini* yoga class in a local gym. When all the other students had left, she said, "I was instructed to give this to you." I looked around. There was no one else in the room, so it had to be me. She presented me with a large owl feather in an even larger box. I wasn't quite sure how to respond to the gift. No one had ever given me a feather in a box before, and certainly not an owl feather. I lifted it up, and I saw dead people jumping up and down, wanting to speak. I quickly put the feather back in the box. In the ensuing months, whenever I lifted the feather up, the same thing happened. A few friends started asking me to get "messages" for them through the feather. I did it for a while, but when friends of friends started to ask, I realized that I was not on earth to be an owl feather channeler, and I thanked the feather, put it away, and went on with my life.

The second feather incident happened with my dear New Zealand friend Christine Bowker Wilson when Paul and I traveled with her family in Europe in three camper vans. We were driving through the countryside when her Maori husband John Wilson, who was sleeping, woke with a start and asked, "Chrissy, isn't this where your grandfather died?" We were passing a road sign with the word Somme on it. "Yes," said Christine. It was in the Battle of the Somme. I never dreamed we'd be going there."

Christine explained that her grandfather's name was James Thomas Bowker. "He was 35 when his body was blown up at the Somme, on July lst, 1916," she said. "My father was his only child and was just six years old when James Thomas was killed. We had photos of him and some personal items and a special plaque about his service in the war. I actually wrote a letter to him and told him I wanted to know more about him, that I loved him and looked forward to meeting him one day. But I hadn't planned to be anywhere near the Somme on this journey."

The World War I Battle of the Somme, a British and French initiative against the Germans in 1916, lasted four months and left an unimaginable one million wounded, maimed, or dead. One of them was Christine's grandfather.

We followed the sign that pointed to a small military museum, and saw a map of all the military cemeteries in the area. I have no idea how this happened, but I pointed to one of them, the Thiepval Memorial, and said we should drive there.

It was almost half an hour out of our way, and I felt concerned that I was leading about twenty-five people, including small babies, on a fruitless, time-consuming chase.

When we arrived at the cemetery, we were overwhelmed by its sheer size, and the thought of the lives cut short and the collective grief of all the families who had lost love ones in one of the bloodiest battles in history. Christine and I saw a monumental arch in the distance, and we walked towards it over an immense, verdant pasture.

Christine looked down and noticed that there was a line of black and white feathers in the grass; they pointed towards the arch. We followed the feathers.

When we stood under the arch, we saw that on either side of us was a large book with the names and addresses of those who were interred in the cemetery. "Which one?" Christine asked. I pointed to the right. She scanned the list, which was in alphabetical order, and under the B's was the name of her grandfather, James Thomas Bowker.

And then my very emotionally controlled girlfriend began to cry. "I knew that one day I would find him," she said.

James Thomas Bowker didn't have a grave, because his body wasn't recoverable. But Christine was, as far as she knew, the only person who had ever visited the cemetery where he was remembered.

All of these experiences that I had were kept as parts of my secret life with the exception of a few close friends. Yes, I wrote a play about it, but that passed as fiction. You can probably understand that talking to the dead was initially not something I shared readily with people. Occasionally I would tell a child who lost a family member about it, and showed her how to connect with the departed through a "*yahrzeit*" candle. I also told several friends, who needed healing with a parent, spouse, sibling, lover, or friend who had died, how to communicate through the candle. A few had troubled relationships, and, in some cases, death had exacerbated the feelings they had when the person was alive. In one case, it was impossible to talk to the person while she was alive, but it became possible after she died. In another instance, the spouse who was left behind discovered very painful secrets about the mate she had lost. He had lied to her, betrayed her, and she was devastated. She was able to communicate with him, vent her anger, and ask for answers.

After the death of my mother, I decided that it was time to break my silence around all things relating to communicating with the dead. A friend and I organized a holiday gathering at his house, and, with his permission, I sent out an email asking the guests to bring a "*yahrzeit*" candle, no matter what their background or religion.

When I walked into the gathering, a woman told me I had something on the back of my black caftan, and she picked it off. A woman sitting next to her said to me, "What is this doing here? It's a white feather." My mother. She showed up at the oddest times and in the most unexpected places. As soon as I saw the feather, all my temerity about what I was about to do vanished.

I told the people at the gathering about my clandestine life of communicating across the great divide. I showed them exactly how I did it with a "*yahrzeit*" candle. And then I asked each of them to find a private place inside or outside of my friend's house, where she or he could light the candle, and talk to a person they had lost. When they were done, I asked them to gather together again in the living room.

Time passed. I wondered if I had made a mistake in organizing this. I wondered how the dispersed people were reacting. And then I stopped wondering because one by one, they came back to the living room.

First, we all sat expectantly. Then each person reported what had happened in the intimacy of her or his communication with a departed loved one. There was deep silence in the room; the silence of people really listening to what others had to say. Some were teary. Others looked relaxed. Or relieved. One or two had a faraway look in their eyes.

Some said they had gotten answers to questions. A few said nothing happened. Others felt a calm presence. Several said they had connected to people they hadn't thought about in years. One or two communicated with multiple people. Each story was moving, compelling, surprising. It made no different where the deceased person lived, or how long ago she or he died. It was like a window had opened up into the soul of each person sitting in the room and we were all allowed to peer inside.

At the end of the evening, I felt as though we had all been on a voyage together that transcended what most people consider to be the end of life. And I was ready to go public. I wrote an article, the response was enormous — hundreds of thousands of readers — and then I figured it was time to write a book about experiences I had had, so that readers would understand that if they wished to communicate with the dead, they were not alone, strange, or going out on an emotional limb; they were simply sharing and participating in what was already being done all around the world.

And now, if you are ready, come with me to the second part of this book where you'll see many ways of doing it.

PART TWO

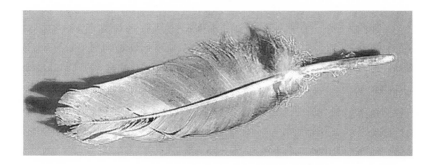

Chapter XXII.

HOW TO COMMUNICATE WITH THE DEAD

In my experience, there are many forms of communication that are possible. They can be life changing and affirming, or expand your universe to include both visible and invisible energies. They may bring up issues you never thought about before. And each of them is a memorable experience and an adventure. Some are bidden, and some are unbidden. In other words, you may contact the dead, or they may initiate the contact with you.

1. Spontaneous contact: It is not something you solicit or ask for. You may be grieving and suddenly you hear a voice speaking to you when you are at the cemetery, as I did, or you see a vision of the deceased sitting on the edge of your bed or in his or her favorite chair. It can also happen while you are brushing your teeth, walking your dog, or loading dish soap into your cart at a market. It may last a short time, happen once, or recur periodically and unpredictably.

It is your choice entirely about how to respond. You may just observe it and feel the comfort and solace it offers. You don't need to do anything else. You just know and feel that the deceased is in contact, and that the relationship still exists no matter how much time has elapsed since the person died. It is an affirmation that death is not the end, and that the person you lost has not stopped caring about you or wanting to make amends.

It may happen at a difficult time in your life, and perhaps you will cry from unhappiness or relief. You can ask the person for help, or request that she come back again. You can also choose to ask a question out loud or in your mind, like, "Am I doing the right thing in life?" or "Should I stay in my marriage?" or "Will my child ever find her way in life?" You may get an answer, or you may not. You may get an answer later on that day, or the next day. The experience is as varied as people are.

It may be a communication from someone in your life who was toxic and destructive to you. Even if it's an apology, you can choose not to respond to it, or to tell the person to go away. If he comes back you can reject the contact again. And again. It's like unfriending someone on social media or blocking his calls. You can think of it as having caller ID on your phone, seeing who the unwanted caller is and choosing not to answer. You control the information you want to come in. It is in your hands. You are not helpless. You may feel vulnerable, but, in fact, you are not. Even if the deceased controlled you in life, you hold the reins once he is gone. If you have ever been on a horse, you know what it means to hold the reins. If you want the horse to start, you give it a gentle but firm kick. If you want him to stop, you pull on the reins. You can signal the horse to turn. If you are afraid of horses, you don't need to ride at all.

2. You may choose to write a letter to someone who has passed. No one ever has to read it, so it has the privacy of a journal entry but

also the possibility that it will be read and received by the addressee. Remember that there is an energy that exists after a person has died. You are tapping into that energy, and writing to a person who was present in your life and is still present in energetic form.

There is no right way to compose the letter; just let your feelings pour out and don't censor them. Write from the heart rather than the head. Write with pen and paper rather than on your tablet or computer; there is power and purpose in forming the letters yourself. The goal of letter writing is to communicate. Don't worry about spelling, grammar, or sentence structure. Write as though no one is looking, no one is judging, and the person you are writing to probably wants or needs to read the letter as much as you want or need to write it.

You may wish to try an automatic writing or psychography. You put pen to paper, and let the letter write itself without trying consciously to compose it. You allow your subconscious mind or spirit to take over.

Another technique is sitting down, putting the pen on the paper, and starting to write without ever pausing or stopping until the letter is done. You never lift the pen from the paper until you have written the last word. It doesn't matter if the letters and words are all connected and there is no space between words. You may wish to do this for as long as you can, then pause, take a few breaths, and set the pen to paper and begin again without ever lifting the pen from the paper. It takes a lot of concentration to do this, so you will be focused on the task and not overthinking the content. It can free you emotionally to say what you want to say even if you never had the courage to do it before. The fact that the letter may not be legible once all the words are connected is a reassurance that no one else will read it besides you and the departed.

However you decide to write the letter, tell the deceased how much you miss him, or how much he hurt you. Do not be afraid to go into detail, as there is no word limit and your letter can be as long as you wish. It can be sentences, paragraphs, or pages. Ask the person for forgiveness for mistakes you made, or ask him to apologize for what he has done to you. Ask if she is okay, and what it is like after death. Ask why she killed herself, or why she gave you up for adoption. Or express your anger and request that he leave you alone, and never contact you again. Your words may be like a prayer, giving thanks or requesting help or intercession.

Once the letter is written you can bury it or burn it. Smoke is said to carry the prayers up to the heavens, or wherever the gods and the deceased reside. Or you may choose to leave it at the graveside of the deceased or near the site of his cremated remains.

3. Pay attention to dreams. Some people are visited at night through dreams in which the dead appear. They may bring you a message or speak to you. They may be much younger than they were when they died, or even younger than they were before you entered their lives and they entered yours. When you wake up, immediately write down the dream in as much detail as you can remember. Think about what the dream may signify, or how it makes you feel. Discuss it with people you trust or with a dream therapist or psychotherapist. You may remember the dream for the rest of your life with the same vividness and clarity that it had when you first awoke after having it. It was likely a comforting dream that you can always keep close to you and access, if you wish. If it was a disturbing dream, you can decipher it and then discard it. You are never helpless and can likely exercise powers and control you never thought you had.

4. Be on the lookout for signs. The dead may communicate to you through a favorite song, a particular flower or bird that appears out of season, the scent of her perfume, or an object suddenly showing up where it wasn't before or moving. You may feel the presence of a loved

one on a holiday or anniversary. It is usually a comforting experience.

I have several friends who repeatedly find objects like dimes, feathers, or pennies when they are in painful or difficult situations. They feel that the departed are trying to help them or soothe their pain. It comforts them to feel the presence and to know the dead are watching over them.

5. Do not be embarrassed to talk to the deceased out loud, any time you wish. You may, of course, do it silently in your head, but there is a certain power in saying and hearing the words spoken out loud. You may hear the response of the dead at once, after a certain time, or not at all. Some people have long, extended conversations. Others just have a feeling that the departed are listening.

6. Many people find it easier to talk to the dead at a cemetery, in front of their tombstone, or to address their picture, which you can set on an altar, on top of a fireplace, or anywhere you wish.

7. The dead who want to communicate can do it in an almost endless number of ways: through a fortune cookie, a sign in front of a church, a mirror, a line of spoken dialogue in a movie, an article in a newspaper, magazine, or online.

8. You may choose to start by simply saying the name of the deceased person aloud. Names are very important. I learned from an ultra-Orthodox Jewish woman that when parents first see their baby, they get a spiritual hit on her or him, and that is the name they give to their child.

Sometimes, when I am giving a talk, I ask attendees to speak the name of an ancestor aloud. Often they begin to cry and they don't know why. Maybe it is the first time since the person's death that his name has been spoken, or perhaps it is the first time the survivor has ever said the name of the ancestor out loud. I have come to believe that when you say the name of the dead, it temporarily gives her a spark of life. I read somewhere that when a dead person's name is no longer mentioned, she passes into oblivion and is forgotten.

9. It's a waste of time and energy to wonder if it's all happening in your imagination or whether you're nuts. When it comes to communicating with the dead, send your logical, rational, limiting mind away on vacation. If you discount your experience, you deprive yourself of a potentially mind-expanding opportunity. It also is a waste of time to keep it a big, dark secret as I did for many years. I could have learned so much from others during that time. I might have found out, as I did years later from a Native American man, that because the eagle flies higher than any other bird, it is closest to the divine and is said to carry our messages. I might have heard, as I did earlier today from a beautiful Mexican woman, that "Mexicans always talk about death. They live with death. I love death. I have no fear of it."

10. Keone Nunes, a Kahuna Kā Uhi or master tattoo practitioner from Hawaii, uses traditional tools to make tattoos. He explained the importance of the tattoos on his own body and their relation to ancestors. "When we pass on, our ancestors recognize us through these patterns and they prepare a seat for us. A seat alongside of them – wherever they are." So besides being body adornments, tattoos can be a connection to those who passed and ensure a place for us when we pass.

Perhaps you have decided, at this point, that you do not want to communicate with the dead. That is fine. Maybe it's not the right time, or maybe there will never be a right time, and that's okay too. There may be humor in the communication, but it is not a parlor game or a form of amusement. It is done because you miss someone, because you need to heal a relationship, because you want answers, desire connection, have things you need to say to the deceased, or because you are grieving.

I have received hundreds of emails from people asking me to help them communicate with someone they lost. Often they ask me outright to be their medium. This book is about how you can do it yourself, without an intermediary.

It is important to remember that when you prepare to initiate communication with the dead, it is an invitation. You welcome the person, and invite her or him to talk. It is like tuning into a channel on TV or radio. If you are communicating with someone who was difficult or even abusive in your life, remember that you are not inviting the person back into your life. There is a big distinction. You desire answers or clarification. You need to know if the person is sorry. You want to ask the person to release you from a curse you have been carrying. You can do whatever you wish. You are simply inviting two-way communication. You control the session. You control what you ask, what you want to know. If the answers are what you do not wish to hear, you can stop the session. And if the person does not want to talk to you, or is not ready for communication, she or he won't show up. Then you can opt to try again another time or not. But I would venture to say that if you are fearful that something bad will happen, either don't do it, or else think about whether this is just fear and imagination talking, and not the truth. Our minds are very powerful in both good and not-so-good ways. They can alter a situation for the better, or they can negatively impact what happens. Take the time to look inward, and see if you are ready and willing to undertake communication, and if it feels safe for you. Maybe just read about it, below, and see how it feels to you. Following any one of the protocols can bring you peace, comfort, connection, answers, and solace. As I indicated early in the book, I do not know anyone who has had an unpleasant experience, except that some were disappointed they couldn't establish a connection. Trust yourself. You will know what to do. If you are worried, fearful or concerned, only do it if you feel safe. If you need advice about whether this is a good idea for you, ask someone who knows you and cares about you, or a professional person you trust. For me, it has always been a positive, soothing, sometimes surprising experience.

If you do want to communicate with the departed as I do, here are exact instructions. Remember that it takes two for this to work: you and the person you have lost. Both have to be willing. And the way I do it is like a ceremony or a ritual.

1) First, go to a supermarket where they sell kosher or Jewish foods. Most large markets carry them, and you will find a selection of edibles like *matzo* and chicken soup. In that section, you will find *yahrzeit* candles. They come in a glass, which can be any size, and there is Hebrew writing on the outside of the glass. They are inexpensive.

If you cannot find a market that carries the candles, check at a synagogue or, if there is one near you, a gift shop that sells Judaica. Sometimes you will have to travel to a town where they sell *yahrzeit* candles. Getting there is part of the process of communicating with the dead. From the moment you decide to buy a candle, you have already started.

If you still cannot locate a candle, then look on the Internet. Multiple sites sell *yahrzeit* candles that come in different kinds of glass, and even in metal. If possible, I recommend the glass kind.

Remember that anyone of any race, religion, nationality, age, size, or shape can do it. I believe it works partially because it burns for 24 hours.

Many people have written to me asking me to make contact with the deceased for them. They have never expended the effort to find a candle, and they think it would be easier to have someone else make the contact. I ask them to get the candle and follow the protocol. If you are unwilling to find the candle, the dead may be unwilling to respond. If this applies to you and makes you smile, fine. It never hurts to smile and have a lighter heart.

2) Find a quiet place in your house, apartment, or dormitory where you can be alone. You may, if you wish, choose to have another person with you, but it has to be someone who will not distract you in any way or insert himself or herself into the communication.

If you decide to do this more than once, you can have a person close to you communicate with your departed. It can bring healing and completion to the person who is doing it. If, for example, a parent or relative hurt you, someone who loves you may want to ask questions and express feelings towards the deceased person who caused you harm. In that case, I suggest that you be a witness to the communication, rather than an active participant. In my experience, communication is successful if one person per session does it.

3) Light the *yahrzeit* candle. Invite the person in. Say her name. Then, speaking out loud, tell the departed person what has been going on in your life since his untimely death. Bring her up to date. Talk as long as you wish and give as much detail as you wish. It is important that you do this out loud. You may become sad as you speak, and you may cry. This is normal.

4) After you have finished speaking, ask the departed questions that can be answered by yes or no. You can ask any questions; there are no restrictions. But remember that the only answers you will get will be yes or no, so frame the questions to elicit those answers.

Questions may be about the deceased, like, "Are you okay?" or "Are you out of pain?" Many deceased people, including those I knew, saw their loved ones come into their rooms in the weeks and days before they passed. You can ask, "Are you united now with your loved ones?" You may ask if they still love you, or if you are safe in your current relationship. You can ask if they think you are on the right career path, or if your health will be okay. You can ask if they are sorry for what they did to you and others while they were alive. You may inquire if the car accident was really an accident, or if it was intentional.

It the answer to a question is yes, the flame will grow larger or move upwards in the glass.

If the answer is no, the flame will move side to side.

The candle movements may be very dramatic, with the flame bouncing up and down, or side to side, or they can be quite subtle. Sometimes the answers come very quickly, and other times you have to be patient.

5) When you are done, thank the departed aloud for coming.

6) Let the candle burn for 24 hours. Some candles can burn up to 26 hours. Make sure there is a plate or aluminum foil underneath the candle, so there is no risk of burning the surface underneath it.

If this doesn't work the first time, try it again. If it doesn't work the second time, it doesn't mean it won't work. Remember, it takes two people to make it happen: you and the deceased. Both have to be willing and ready.

I wish you well. I wish you very well. I do not know for certain what happens after death. I do not know exactly where the souls or spirits of the dead are. But I know, and what I know has been expanded and amplified by everything I learned from people and cultures around the world, that the dead are accessible to us, as we are to them. The modalities are different, but communication with the dead is a normal part of life for large swaths of the human population. It has persisted for thousands of years because it has benefitted, soothed, and brought connection and meaning to people everywhere.

And now I invite you to experience the communication for yourself. You have many choices of how to do it, and now you know how to contact those who came before you. You can do it. You really can do it. Take a deep breath and try.

ADDENDUM
If You Want To Know More

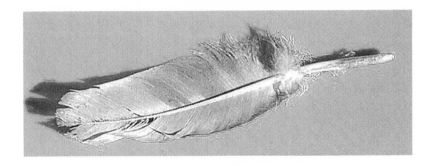

Chapter XXIII.

YOU AND YOUR ANCESTORS

For most people I know, all those *begats* in the Hebrew Bible are a big bore, and they skip right over them. Mizraim begot Ludim, Anamim, Lehabim, Naphtuhim. Who cares? The truth is, I cared. For some odd reason, even as a child, I was mesmerized by the fact that people once knew all their ancestors, right back to Abraham. I didn't know who my grandparents' parents or grandparents were, and I knew precious little about my grandparents.

By the age of 10, I would beg my parents to take me to my grandmother's house, so I could ask her questions about her life before she came to America. I carried with me a pad and pencil, and I scrupulously wrote the answers down. I wanted to know about her village in Russia—what they ate and wore and how they worshipped, mourned, and healed. I begged her to tell me about how she learned to dance and when she was first attracted to a boy and how many hours she worked every day picking tobacco leaves in a field. I grilled her about her parents and her grandparents.

I suppose you could say that my early interviewing was important, because when I met Paul's parents for the first time and asked them about their origins, I found out that his ancestors and mine came from the same tiny village. We were not only connected in this life, but back through time.

When my father died, my mother had her wedding ring made into a pendant, which I wear around my neck. When my grandmother passed away, I asked for her wedding ring, and it has never left the fourth finger of my right hand. On my left hand, I wear my own wedding ring. So when someone asks me about my jewelry, I can tell them that it represents three generations; quite literally, I carry my ancestors with me wherever I go. I find that it strengthens me to be connected back through time.

When I first went to New Zealand, I was stunned to find that every Maori person I met knew the name of the canoe his ancestors had arrived in, over a thousand years ago. And a Maori historian named Porotu, his face covered with ancestral tattoos, recited his lineage back across the great oceans of the world, for thousands of years. As he connected to the ancient ones, as he talked about them, he seemed to grow in power and stature. He knew who he was and where he came from. It gave him a foundation so solid that I had the impression nothing could throw him off balance or knock him over. And, in addition to his ancestors, he spoke about his tribal land that was sacred to his people. Maori people also have a deep sense of place.

I began to think about how we Americans generally identify ourselves. When someone asks about us, we state our name, of course, and, most often, what we do for a living. But what if we lose our job and are unemployed? What happens when we retire? What is our self-definition then? I suddenly felt that our universe is very small and contracted when we are only identified by our current lives. Unlike Porotu, we have nothing to lean on, no one to look back to, and no permanent sense of place or connection to what came before us. And, one day, when our children and grandchildren are gone, if we have any, then it will be as though we never existed.

I have asked people from countries as diverse as Nigeria, Tunisia, Thailand, Micronesia, French Polynesia, and Guatemala about their connection to those that came before them, and it seems as much a part of their lives as eating, sleeping, shopping, and going to work. They know who they are because they know where they come from. They acknowledge and thank those whose shoulders they stand on, who passed on their genes, culture, heritage and wisdom. It is as unthinkable for them to neglect the ancestors, as it is to neglect to put on clothes or comb their hair.

Of course you can do DNA tests that tell you about your ancestors in terms of percentages and places on a map. But besides doing genealogy, there are also ways to connect to the actual people, and who they were. Once you know about them, you can choose to connect to them for solace, comfort, wisdom and the foundation that your personal past provides. And, of course, like all kinds of deep learning, the process itself is a voyage filled with mystery and magic.

Unless most or all members of your family are gone, there are many things you can do to connect to those who came before you. While your relatives are still alive, ask them questions. Make a list of everything you want to know about their lives before you knew them; ask about their parents, grandparents, and great grandparents. Make the questions detailed and specific. It doesn't matter if your antecedents were fabulous or foolish, judges or criminals. The more you know about them, the more you know about you, and the easier it will be to connect to what and who came before you.

Write down everything you learn. It is part of your precious ancestral database.

If you wear your parents' or grandparents' rings, pendants, or watches, you are carrying your heritage with you and honoring the folks who gave you life. If you have a bare wall or empty photo album and family pictures, you can create a photo gallery of the folks who gave you life, and who passed on their genes to you. You will look into their eyes and connect to where you come from, deeply. If you hang the pictures in your home, the connection will happen daily. You will begin to know them, and at any point you can choose to try to communicate with them…or not.

A long time ago, in Kaikoura, New Zealand, the leader of Maori Tours introduced himself to the six people on the tour by telling us the name of his tribal river and mountain. At the end of the tour, he asked each of us to identity ourselves by our mountain and river. At first we were nonplussed, but when we began to think about it, we found that we each had a body of water and a hill that was important to us. A Japanese woman burst out crying when she realized that her last name was the name of a river, and she had never paid attention to it.

What is your river or body of water? Perhaps it is the Mississippi or the East River or Lake Superior; it may be the Nile, Lac Leman, Lake Atitlan, or the Volga, but there is a body of water that defines, geographically, where you come from. And what is the nearest mountain? If you live in Manhattan, it may be a mountain near the town where you grew up, or a peak near your favorite vacation spot, or perhaps Jebel Musa or Mount Sinai. Try presenting yourself to people by acknowledging these two natural elements of your personal world. It will open up a deep and memorable discussion about where they come from too.

If you enjoy traveling, your past is a plane ticket away. Go to the place your ancestors came from. Arm yourself with as much information as possible, but, even if you know nothing more than the name of the place, wander the countryside, talk to people, look at the tombstones. It is your ancestral home.

Your religious or tribal history is also your history. If you are Hindu, Celtic, Sikh, Jewish, Muslim, Buddhist, or Spiritual Baptist, and whether you are practicing or not, when you learn the history, beliefs, migrations, spirituality, triumphs, and sufferings of your people it will connect you to what came before you and give you a sense of your place as a link in a long chain.

When Paul returned to the United States after his ceremony with the Zulu *sangoma* in South Africa, he followed her instructions for deepening his connections to his ancestors. He made a party according to the *sangoma's* instructions. He still wore the piece of red yarn draped around his body like a bandolier, as he had been instructed to do in South Africa. Then we went outside to the gate of our house, holding candles, and he spoke aloud, inviting his ancestors to participate in his life. He only knew a few names, so he sent out a generic invitation. Then, inside the house, he had many candles burning. He provided great food and the ambience was upbeat. When the eating was done, he added a ceremony of his own, that he felt he wanted to do. He invited his friends to sit in a circle and talk about family members they had lost, and to address those people by name. He provided kleenex. For the first time, he and his friends spoke publicly and directly to their deceased parents, grandparents, aunts, and uncles who had been central to their lives. It was as though the ancestors had come to the party, and were there, present, in the room. And, as requested by the *sangoma*, he wore the red yarn for many months.

It surprised me that Paul made this ceremony, as it is not the kind of thing he had done before or has done since. But if you ask him about it, I am sure he will tell you it was meaningful for him, and it was the first time in his life he had felt any link to his ancestors.

If you can, and if you are willing, go to a graveyard where your ancestors are buried and talk to the deceased. Out loud, if you aren't self-conscious, or silently, if you are. Tell your great grandfather who you are, and about your life. Then ask a question or two. Listen deeply. You may be surprised to hear answers. If you do not, just enjoy the connection to those who came before you; it's what cemeteries are for.

When you feel alone, ailing, failing, helpless, hopeless, or stuck, invoke one of your ancestors or all of your ancestors, and ask for help. Ask them to enter your life and tell you what to do, where to go, or how to get unstuck. Then just listen. That's all you need to do. And don't forget to thank the ancestors for all they have passed on to you and for giving you a sense, every hour of every day, that you are deeply connected and never alone.

You now know different ways to connect to and communicate with the dead. Best of luck to you. I know you can do it.

Chapter XXIV.

INVITING COMMUNICATION

This is a very short chapter. It is about what you can do to encourage your loved ones to be available for communication after they are physically gone from their bodies.

It may be excruciating to watch a person close to you die. Even if they have been suffering terribly and they are ready to be free from their ailing bodies, there is something that seems so final about death. But "seems" is the operative word. "Seems" is not the same as "is."

I hope that by now you can entertain the notion that death is not final, and that highly sophisticated and evolved ancient and modern cultures around the world know this and incorporate it into their lives and their belief systems. They are not bound by a finite notion of life and death. They do not see humans as separate from nature, from animals, from life beyond the death of the body.

The person who is passing from this life is getting ready for a very important voyage. It may seem like she is just lying there, but her body, mind, and soul are in deep preparation mode. It is hard for her to leave you, but she must soon go.

The gentlest and best way to proceed is to ask permission. "May I ask you a question?"

She will most likely nod, or say yes.

Then you can ask, "Will you send me a sign from the beyond? Something to let me know that you are there?"

She may not know what to say. This may be foreign territory to her, and something she hasn't thought about. Maybe she doesn't even believe it can happen. But you can give tender suggestions.

"How about feathers? Maybe a specific type of bird? Maybe heads-up pennies lying in my path?"

If she responds, then you have a plan.

If she doesn't respond, you can make a few more suggestions, or you can ask another question.

"Have you ever had a sign or a feeling from someone you love who passed?"

Perhaps she will say that she has heard a special song at an unexpected time or place. Or she will say she once felt a hand on her shoulder. If she can't talk easily, or if she has never had an experience, you can make a specific request.

"Will you please come to me through lights that flicker on and off, or the number 8?"

Your request can be arcane or mundane; it makes no difference. It makes no difference if she agrees, says nothing, or pooh-poohs the whole thing. It makes no difference if you have a great, decent, or troubled relationship. It makes no difference if you are not there, at her bedside, or you ask on the phone. It doesn't even matter if she can no longer talk, and you ask someone to hold the phone up to her ear.

What is important is that you have asked. And once she is gone, it is too late to ask.

After your beloved has died, all you have to do is wait, and stay alert. It may take hours, days, weeks, or months. Please be patient. And when it happens, you will know it. You will just know.

Chapter XXV.

HOW OTHERS HAVE COMMUNICATED WITH THE DEAD

I have received many emails from people who told me about their experiences with communicating with the deceased. I am including a few of them here, and also several that illustrate the kinds of questions people ask. I hope they inspire you.

My family "sees dead people." I have since I was a toddler, not as often now though. Two of my kids do too. There was even a boy that the kids would see running through the yard when they were young, and we'd hear him crying. His name was Curtis, and we searched for him online. He died in the 1950's and we think he probably lived at our house years ago. It was just a normal part of life for us. My grandson used to see angels flying over his grandma's head when he was a toddler.

Frank Cole

When I was a kid if someone was going to die, I would see them before they passed. My father died when I was nine, and two weeks before he passed I saw him walk in my bedroom, but he looked old. I ran downstairs and told him to stop scaring me, and my mother said he hadn't moved from where he was. Then after he died, I heard him at my grandmother's house, telling me to run. He called me Sissy and I heard his voice say "Sissy run," so I ran. I think he didn't want me to see him and be more scared. Then as an adult, every time I was pregnant he would show up. I saw him when I was pregnant with Renee, Renee saw him when I was pregnant with Jeff, and Jeff saw him when I was pregnant with Toby. They'd never seen his photo, they were toddlers but they described exactly how he looked.

Maggie McCabe

I communicate with the deceased and have for many years. My initial contact with spirits started at a young age and was very traumatic (it was continuous for around one year). Western culture does not recognize this ability and is quick to dismiss the possibility as mental illness. I managed to suppress this talent/phenomena and live without speaking about such things for several decades. Approximately six years ago the spirits themselves decided to approach me rather forcefully. At first I thought that I might be suffering from a mental illness, but the idea vanished when I requested proof of the spirits' existence and they delivered it.

I tried to find another experienced communicator to help me understand what was occurring, but my search was not successful. Luckily, the spirits themselves trained me and guided me though this period. This gift is normally kept secret, although on occasion I have relayed messages to friends of love ones who have passed and let them know of their loved ones' presence. My reality is very different from those around me and only a few are aware of my ability. Shamanistic readings are comforting as I see that others like me do exist.

William

My 35-year-old son, Skyler, is dying from brain cancer. He has a wife and a one-month-old son. I hope to be able to give him hope that he can "speak" from the other side. What would I communicate to him now? He may or may not be open to it, but I thought I'd ask. Thank you.

Deanna

I have twice used the candle to communicate with David and will do that again. On the first anniversary of his passing David communicated with me. I didn't want to be alone that day and a good friend came over. I took out a box with some of the umpteen photos I had taken of David over the years and as we were looking at the photos we noticed that a large framed picture on the wall had suddenly moved some two inches to the right. There had not been an earthquake. No one banged on the outside wall of the house behind the photo. There was no reason whatsoever for the picture to move on its own. We knew that it was David.

I left the photo askew for about a week and then asked David if I could put it back. The candle flamed up.

Thanks for letting me know about the candle. I will also try it with my parents who are long gone.

Jan Bauman

I really wish I could get some help. My grandma passed away in 2012. Because of my parents I was not able to attend her death ceremony. My grandma was not just my grandma… she was mother to me … I spent my whole childhood with her and I grew up with her, and my parents separated me from her. Please would u help me to reach out to her ... I wanna hear her or ask a few questions.

Name Withheld

My name is Nashaye and I'm 17 years old. I received your book "Life is a Trip" and enjoyed it but had a few questions. First, I lost my mom when I was 12 years old, a couple of days before my birthday. My mother has been visiting me in my dreams and mostly it has been memories. But at 5 a.m., I was awakened by something tickling my ear. My mind and bodystate were awake but I didn't open my eyes. Then I heard my mom call my name. Her voice was light and sounded like a whisper. I managed to understand what she was saying. I asked "Mom is that you?" she said "Yes," then I asked "Is this real and is this a gift?" she said "Yes." I then was having a conversation with her in my head. It was like I asked her something or told her something and I could hear her voice beside me. To fast forward I then said to her "Everything's been OK except you know me and aunt don't get along. I just feel like I always mess up something or do something wrong." I started crying while I had my eyes closed. Then I felt the left side of my bed sink in as if someone was sitting there. Then I felt a light hand and arm around me as if someone was hugging and comforting me. She then said "You'll be okay" and then that presence left and she said, "We can start meeting like this and I'll be waiting for you tomorrow and whenever you need me." So I was wondering could you tell me the exact steps on what to do like step by step with the candle. Please reply back.

Neshaya Brazziel

The first time I remember actually seeing and hearing from the other side was when I found out that my biological father, who passed when I was six months old, had gotten run over by a car on his way to work. My son was about two years old and I was in the military stationed in Puerto Rico, and it was one of those feelings when we find ourselves awake but kind of paralyzed in a dream state but knowing we are really awake…but just in relaxed state. Around 5 a.m. I saw a man very vividly (the color of his hair, the suit he was wearing, etc.). At the time I thought it was my grandfather because I had never met my father, who died at the age of 30. He looked a bit like a photo that I saw of my grandfather (my mom's dad) but his message was nothing that my grandfather would say. I passed the message to my mother (it was for her) and he was apologizing for leaving her with two small children and saying how much he loved her. I said to him, "What are you talking about?" and I was disagreeing with him—my 22 year old self—LOL. He just totally ignored me and continued to talk like he only had a certain timeframe to speak and pass his information. When I told my mom and explained what he looked like and what he was wearing she knew immediately who it was…but for some odd reason she let me figure it out for myself, which I did :). When the light came on I told her "Oh it was Mike, my dad" and she said, "Yes, I know."

Tammyanne

From the moment Dreidel entered my life she was special. At her dog naming party she practically named herself. Sitting in the center of fifteen of my college buddies, she started twirling around, chasing her tail.

"She looks like a little Dreidel (spinning top)" someone yelled out. And so it was. Many years passed. She traveled with me. She went everywhere with me. She lived with me in New York City and St. Louis, Missouri. One day at work I sensed something was wrong. I left work to run home, and she was sitting at the door, breathing heavily. Her eighteen years had been filled with mostly great times we'd had together. I phoned the Vet and put her on the speakerphone. He asked me to bring her in. I intuitively knew what he meant. I sat on the floor with her, crying. After ten minutes she sat up straight in front of me and put her paw on my shoulder as if to say, "Let's go. It's time." We took a cab to the office and yes, it was determined that her lungs and heart were filling with fluid. It was time. I brought her ashes home in a flowered tin that I kept in a corner of my big wooden hutch.

One day I took the tin out to just sit and hold her. I silently communicated that this was a short visit. She communicated back, through that intuitive voice, that she needed more time with me. The moment was very disconcerting and confusing. But I didn't listen to her and replaced the tin and her ashes in its corner. All of a sudden there was a loud crash. My sister, who was on the other end of the phone, said, "What was that!?" As I walked back into the living room I saw that the top of the tin had blown off and broken a plate on the other side of the shelf. So I took Dreidel out of the hutch and sat with her as she had requested of me in the first place.

Barry Woodstock

We went through the process of Larry's execution three times. I was present as a Spiritual Advisor. One time he was strapped in with about five minutes to go when the call from the Governor's office came in, "We've got a stay" he announced. So, the execution did not take place. That night, at least. I visited frequently with Larry. He had a love of animals that went very deep. We spoke a lot about the dogs and cats in our lives.

The day came when Larry's execution went through. Lethal injection. I have witnessed and worked with men who faced both.

A few days after Larry's execution a beautiful Labrador Retriever showed up in the woods across the street from my house. He perked up when he saw me but would not come to me. Then, as quickly as he appeared, he disappeared. The next day he came again. I could see him through the dense pine trees. And I could feel his energy directed at me. This went on for a week until that day that he slinked across the street and lay down at my feet.

"Who are you?" I queried. He let me pet him. He wagged his tail. He licked my cheeks. I sat in the grass with him. Petted him. Praised him.

And then he disappeared. Never to be seen again. I asked him if he was Larry. He just wagged and licked as if saying thank you. He appeared as his cherished childhood dog that he had told me about. He was saying "Thank you" and telling me he was OK.

Jane Davis

I must always carry a bottle of water with me wherever I go. I can't remember when this obsession began, but it's been many decades. Because of the real possibility of dry throat or choking, satisfying this need seemed a simple and reasonable thing to do. I didn't give it much thought... until a session with a shaman in Santa Fe, New Mexico.

In the hope of increasing my intuitive abilities, I was working with this shaman and making progress in feeling, seeing and sensing beyond the obvious, and coming to trust my perceptions. One day, while in trance, I became agitated by the image of a woman walking in a dry riverbed, obviously in distress. She had brown skin and a tattered dress and I sensed she was desperately seeking water, but there was none to be found. It seemed she and two young children, a boy and a girl, had left their tribe in search of water and wandered into the desert where both children died, and she also died of thirst and a broken heart. Her mother, the grandmother of the children, had stayed behind with the clan and survived. After days and weeks of waiting the return of her beloveds, she knew they had died of thirst. Her grief was beyond measure.

Later that day I returned home and sensed a presence in the yard. It was the spirit of the grieving grandmother. Her anguish was palpable.

I spoke directly to the sorrowful energy of the grandmother and felt her draw nearer. I assured her that her children were safe and gone, and she was free to join them. I waited, gently repeating words of comfort. Suddenly I heard a whooshing sound and felt her energy disappear, like a person rushing out of a burning building toward safety. She had gone with relief and I felt that too, and I cried. Perhaps my experience has mythological roots in the Mexican folk tale of La Llorona, a weeping woman who must spend eternity wandering the earth in search of her children, which she had drowned in a moment of jealousy. But, whatever the source, the sound and feeling of the released spirit of the agonized grandmother were real to me. And I still carry a bottle of water with me wherever I go.

Aysha Griffin

Something odd happened after Mom died. When my father died when I was nine years old, I found a dime on the ground at his funeral so I pushed it into his grave spot. I've found countless pennies since then, but never a dime. Then the day after Mom passed, I looked down and I found a dime. I think that's Mom's way of letting me know that she's still with me. I saved this dime :)

Margie Baxley

After my mother's stroke in 2008 she told us that she saw heaven when she was in a coma for four hours. I was sitting by her, whispering not to leave me. We even had a priest do the last rites and the kids all came and told her goodbye, as they didn't expect her to make it through the night. Then she opened her eyes.

She couldn't talk but a few weeks later, with her letter board she told us about her time in the coma. She told us how beautiful and peaceful Heaven was – no pain. Then she felt a hand on her shoulder and the voice told her she had to go back because I still needed her.

Then she opened her eyes and we had her for almost 10 years. She even described the room the kids were waiting in and everyone who was in that room. She'd never seen that room before but she described it and even how the kids were sitting.

Alicia Swann

My father-in-law had been sick for months and was declining day by day. We knew it was just a matter of time and were waiting for the phone call that would have us all headed up to the far north of Japan to hopefully see him before he died, or at least be there for the family and the very prolonged and elaborate funeral. Unfortunately, I also had a trip back to England booked to see my very sick dad and my father-in-law had insisted that if he were to die whilst we were away, we were not to fly back.

We received the news during a stop over in Dubai and whilst it was a relief to know that my father-in-law was finally at peace and the waiting was over, it was sad to know that we would not be able to say a "proper" goodbye. The feeling of unfinished business persisted until three days later whilst FaceTiming with my husband (who was at the family home in Japan). My husband was explaining the arrangements and holding the phone up so we could say hello to all the gathered friends and relations. In the background we could see the coffin. Being a curious sort I asked my husband if we could have a closer look—it was my first time to see a Japanese coffin and it is an impressive thing. Decorated in white and silver it looks like nothing so much as the kind of deep freeze in a grocery store that holds all the ice-creams, although instead of finding a cornetto when my husband slid back the lid, we saw my father-in-law packed in dry ice. He looked peaceful and completely not-present as my husband leant in and patted his cheek. I called my boys over and after they had instructed my husband to slide the lid open and closed a few times, we said goodbye to 'oji-san' (grandfather), said goodbye to the family and proceeded to have our

English summer BBQ with a sense of peace and closure. I like to think that my father-in-law would have found the episode rather amusing. I wouldn't say that I heard anything from inside the coffin, but after that call I felt peaceful and that I had done what needed to be done. My husband was also happy that we had all said goodbye.

Julia Maeda

Having lost my parents when I was a child I have a unique acquaintance with death. In my private practice as a mental health counselor I work with fatherless and motherless individuals. Frequently I'm able to open to the lost parent. I receive information about the family and how to help my clients heal from the grief of their loss.

On my 54th birthday I danced Argentine tango until 2 a.m. Then I drove the 60 miles from New York City to my Red Bank, New Jersey apartment. At 4 a.m. as I sat on the edge of my bed pulling on my pajamas a hand stroked my forehead. My mother had died 44 years before and yet I had never forgotten her touch. For a moment we connected. Then she was gone. A precious 54th birthday gift.

Andrea Campbell

Mom died in 2009. By that time, I had been a Hospice nurse for 10 years, and it was clear that Mom was not going to recover from the bleeding within her brain. I flew down to Florida to care for her, get her onto the Hospice program and give my then 88-year-old Father a break.

I was on the bed with Mom, and I put my arms around her and said, "Mom, you will never be forgotten. The stories about you have been handed down from your children to grandchildren, and will continue to be handed down to great grands and great great grands and on. Mom, you will never be forgotten." At that moment, her breathing changed and I called Dad and Tina to the bedside and we held her hands and stroked her gently until she took her last breath moments later.

The day of her death was full of activities, phone calls, making arrangements etc. But it was the next day that a deep sadness and grieving overtook me, as I went for a long walk in their retirement village. I was walking and sobbing with an almost unbearable ache in my heart. Suddenly something inexplicable happened: as I was walking and crying and feeling this pain, I suddenly felt the distinct sensation of a left arm come around my waist, and a right hand hold onto my left hand, as though someone was walking by my side, making this loving gesture. The sensation was so distinct that I turned my head to the right, saying to the vacant space, "Mom, is that you?" I did not hear an answer except that I continued to feel this sensation all the way back to Dad's house, about a quarter of a mile away.

Bee Zollo

Great blue herons were a symbol of connection in my family long before my dad suddenly passed. Throughout my childhood we saw them on Jewish holidays in our "Temple of Nature" out on the lake. After he died, my mom and I saw at least one every time we walked to the lake near our house. She would always say she felt these birds were a sign from my dad.

About four years after my dad's passing, my bosses invited me onto their sailboat. I found myself thinking and sharing about my dad more than I thought I would – he loved sailing. He felt so present with me. I wished I could be sharing this experience with him. As we were driving the boat back to the dock, slowly turning into my bosses' space, I looked up and lost my breath. There, seemingly waiting on the wooden dock, directly in the middle of the open slip, was a great blue heron. One of the grumpiest and wisest looking ones I'd ever seen. I had this deep feeling that it was my dad telling me he was there, in a different form, with me out on the water and always.

Daisy Stelzer

I was celebrating Purim at the Santa Fe, New Mexico Jewish Center, Chabad, in the spring of 2018, two years after having unexpectedly received a divine instruction to "move to Israel." By then I had a plane ticket to Israel with a 10-hour stopover in New York.

As I passed by the table where the Rabbi's son, Mendel Levertov, a rabbinical student in New York, was sitting, he looked up at me and said, "It is more important to go to New York than to Israel." He explained that I should go to the *ohel* (gravesite) of the Rebbe (the late Menachem Mendel Schneerson), where people can ask a question of him and where some get an answer.

So I went to the *ohel* during my stopover, wrote my question on a paper and put it in an enclosed 10-foot-square area (among about a million other papers) in front of the gravestones of the Rebbe and his wife—and I got an answer. My question was: "Is moving to Israel the right thing for me to do?" Immediately I experienced these words: "YES! And the details will unfold after you get there."

I needed no more assurances. I arrived in Israel, where I stayed for seven weeks at a yeshiva in the Old City of Jerusalem. It was a "pilot trip." Now, five months later, I am almost complete with the process of Aliyah (requesting Israeli citizenship). Soon I will be back in Jerusalem, where I will be living in a small apartment in the especially religiously observant neighborhood of Mea Shearim. I won't need a car. Grocery stores, a pharmacy and a synagogue for study are across the street. Baruch HaShem.

Richard Freeman

My late first husband, David, an astrophysicist, passed away after a seven and a half year battle with a rare spinal cord cancer that ultimately took over his entire central nervous system. The genuinely valiant battle ended after a day of coma, at home, in home-hospice, as I held him.

The day before he lapsed into coma, Judie asked whether I hoped to maintain contact with David's soul, and when I said, "Of course I do," she told me that I would need to tell him so. So, as his consciousness faded I stroked his head and said quietly that when he needed to leave, he should feel free to do so, but that I wanted his soul to remain in contact with me.

Within hours of his death, lights in the house turned on and off as though of their own volition and the electrical power (only in our house) began to flicker unaccountably. About ten days after his death, as I was sitting in the same family room that had been our hospice, speaking with my friend, D., about her grandchildren, I suddenly saw him—transparent, but in full color, dressed in one of his favorite shirts—sitting at the edge of a futon in the same part of the room where he had died, smiling gently at me as I told our friend about seeing him. After perhaps a minute, the image vanished. A couple of weeks later I heard a noise in the basement; a few hours later I went down to investigate and found that one of a group of champagne bottles that had been standing upright and undisturbed for some months, had burst—David had always laughed at me for keeping a bottle or two of champagne around ready for any celebration. There was a round puddle of wine around the base of the bottle; the neck was broken off, and rested on the floor beside it. If shaken, maybe a champagne bottle might explode, but this neat arrangement defied the laws of physics. As I examined the broken glass, I heard his voice saying sadly, "There's nothing to celebrate."

In the nine years since, I have often sensed him looking through my eyes at family events, felt he was communicating with me when I heard several pieces of classical music important to us played in succession on the radio, and frequently find my eyes turning, for no reason, to look at a digital clock, or other numerical read-out, to find the screen showing one of several numbers important to our family. I've been joyfully remarried for some years now, our family is thriving and life is full of happiness, yet I hope David's presence will always be near.

Honeybee

My grandson was born a year after my husband died. He has his grandfather's eyes and when he first looked at me in that unfocused way that newborns do, suspended between this world and the one beyond, I felt a jolt of recognition. With each passing year, I see more of a resemblance to his grandfather, as do my family and friends. After forty-two years of marriage I was well aware of my husband's personality, his little gestures, funny quirks. Perhaps that's why I'm so quick to recognize them in this child. I know the resemblance is in part genetic, and in part attributable to the limited range of human emotions and behavior. My grandson is very much his own person. Yet I also believe his grandfather has reached across the divide to embrace this child he would have cherished and to give him and our family the gift of a part of himself, and his undying love.

Dorty Nowak

In December 2017, at the age of 93, my father had a peaceful passing. In addition to having been a member of a local synagogue for over 70 years, he had been active in many Jewish organizations. Although I lived in New Mexico and my one sibling lived in Oregon, over the years we took turns going to be with him, particularly during the Jewish High Holy Days. Those occasions with my dad were, for the most part, my only times attending religious services. This year (2018), I wanted to honor my dad during the High Holy Days. I attended services, including one specifically oriented towards honoring those who had passed.

During the service, I felt as if I heard my father say, in effect, "I know this isn't your thing. You've done good. You don't need to keep doing this." Although it sounded like him and the words were ones he would use, I wasn't sure if this was what I wanted to hear, or if I had had a communication from my dad. Further reflection and checking with myself (which included a technique called "muscle checking" that I have used for years to slip past my conscious thinking mind and see what was true for me) confirmed that I had, as far as I could tell, received a message from him.

A.O. Adleman

Oh Judie...You gave me back my light at the end of the tunnel.
How can I say thank you for saving me today? Words are...inadequate.

I had to talk to him. I had no way to get the special candle. My friend had given me several boxes of the small Chanukah candles. I used the blue. It was Randy's favorite color.

I cried so hard, but he understood! He was here! He talked to me. We talked until the candle burned down. He is with me now.

How can I say thank you for saving me? It was like he was waiting to hear from me in this way.

I have talked to him many times now. He comforts me and is waiting for me.

With a lighter heart, I thank you.

Elizabeth Tennis

Congratulations on writing your new book! Spirit communication has opened up such a whole new interesting world for me. Mostly it's been a positive experience for me but like everything it does have its tough moments. I'm still learning the basics.....I can't hear them but I feel them and see them. I communicate with them by numbers and them also spelling things out. At first I thought I was losing it big time…I saw angels too…there is so much more I can share with you! I really just wanted to find someone who will understand where I'm coming from ya know? Maybe to keep myself from thinking I'm going crazy!

Karen

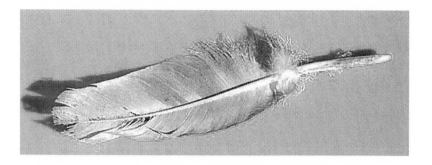

Chapter XXVI.

THINGS TO THINK ABOUT

OR DISCUSS

H ave you ever had an experience with communication from someone who died? If so, what happened?

Do you believe there is life after death? Reincarnation?

Does your religion, spiritual affiliation, or any other group you belong to or family member teach you that you cannot or should not communicate with the dead?

Are you afraid of communicating with someone you have lost? If so, why?

Did you try the protocol described in this book for connecting with someone you have lost? If so, what happened?

Do you feel comfortable talking about communication with the dead with other people? If not, why not? If you have done it, what was the reaction of others?

Would you like someone to contact you after you die? Why or why not?

Have you ever derived comfort from visiting someone's grave? If so, what happened?

Have you ever gone to a ceremony in another country where people honored their dead? What was your reaction?

Have you ever dreamed about someone you know who died? What happened in the dream?

ABOUT THE AUTHOR

Judith Fein is an award-winning international travel journalist who lives to leave. She resided for more than ten years in North Africa and Europe, where she ran an experimental theatre company and was an actor and director. She is an alumna of the Sundance Institute and worked as a film and television writer in Hollywood for more than twelve years. She has had ten plays produced in the U.S. and Europe, and *Visiting Dad*, a short play about communicating with the dead, has been performed around the world. She was the recipient of a grant from Opera America to create the libretto for the enthusiastically reviewed opera *Hotel Eden* with composer Henry Mollicone. With her extensive background in writing, film, and all aspects of performance, Judith writes reviews and articles about theatre, opera, film, dance, and art.

Judith also lives to learn. She has a passion for adventures that are exotic, authentic, quirky, historic, and immersed in local culture. She has written travel articles for more than one hundred prominent magazines, newspapers, blogs, and Internet sites, and won awards for her books and many published pieces. She was a regular reporter for "The Savvy Traveler" on public radio, is a frequent guest on radio shows, and is often interviewed as a travel expert. She is the executive editor and co-founder, with Ellen Barone, of the popular website https://www.YourLifeisaTrip.com. Judith is an acclaimed speaker for many venues and is known for her informative, humorous, and inspirational talks and workshops on a wide variety of subjects. She blogs for Psychology Today about Transformative Travel, for the Santa Fe Opera about operas for beginners, and is the Senior Travel Correspondent for the San Diego Jewish Journal. She is a member of the Society of American Travel Writers. With her photojournalist husband Paul Ross, she does travel talks and performances. The duo has taught travel writing and photography around the world.

Judith's website is: https://www.Globaladventure.us

To watch Judith's TEDx talk about Deep Travel: https://www.youtube.com/watch?v=GErjagMyrYk&feature=youtu.be

Other books by Judith Fein:

LIFE IS A TRIP: The Transformative Magic of Travel

THE SPOON FROM MINKOWITZ: A Bittersweet Roots Journey to Ancestral Lands

ACKNOWLEDGEMENTS AND THANKS

For Paul Ross, who is my everything and who has shared these extraordinary experiences with me. He has his head in the stars, his feet firmly planted on the ground, and his eyes positioned behind his camera lens whenever subjects appear.

For Aysha Griffin, my cheerleader on this book from inception to completion, and Louise Rubin, whose keen librarian eye has been invaluable throughout the process. Thank you both for your open hearts.

For Margie Baxley with GeekWebsites.com, who lovingly, caringly, transformed my manuscript into a book.

For Anne Clark, who created the cover with patience, creativity, and love.

For Phyllis Wolf, who speaks truth to writers.

For my friends and colleagues for their suggestions and support.

For all those mentioned in the book who shared their lives, culture, and wisdom. I am deeply grateful.

For the early readers, who generously endorsed my book.

And for you, the reader, who is always with me when I am traveling and then writing.

A NOTE FROM
THE AUTHOR:

You may have read some parts of this in *LIFE IS A TRIP*. The Transformative Magic of Travel, *THE SPOON FROM MINKOWITZ*, or some of my articles. But most of it I have never written about and some of it I have not even spoken about.

Made in the USA
Coppell, TX
09 December 2019